I0135514

THE TRUMP REVOLUTION

THE
TRUMP
REVOLUTION

A NEW ORDER OF GREAT POWERS
ALEXANDER DUGIN

ARKTOS
LONDON 2025

ΛRKTOS

Arktos.com fb.com/Arktos arktosmedia arktosjournal

Copyright © 2025 by Arktos Media Ltd.

All rights reserved. No part of this book may be reproduced or utilised in any form or by any means (whether electronic or mechanical), including photocopying, recording or by any information storage and retrieval system, without permission in writing from the publisher.

ISBN
978-1-917646-44-4 (Paperback)
978-1-917646-29-1 (Hardback)
978-1-917646-30-7 (Ebook)

Translation
Cyrus Longworth

Editing
Constantin von Hoffmeister

Layout
Tor Westman

CONTENTS

TRUMP'S VICTORY OVER THE LIBERAL HORROR

by Constantin von Hoffmeister

T HE WORLD ENDED. It ended in a neon blizzard, an electric storm of shattered paradigms. The so-called "elite," the architects of decay, the Davos puppeteers who had sculpted the 21st-century dystopia, were left exposed as charlatans. Their grand vision of a global technocratic utopia had crumbled under the weight of its own contradictions, suffocated by its hubris, drowning in the grotesque spectacle of its own design. And from the debris, from the desecrated corpses of the globalist priests, from the burning libraries of Davos, emerged the Trump Revolution. But hadn't we been here before? The first apocalypse. The first betrayal. The first ascension. The first crucifixion of a man with golden hair and a mouth that devoured entire civilizations. My book *Esoteric Trumpism* (Arktos, 2024) foresaw it: the conjuring of the political sorcerer, the oracular tweets as Enochian scripture, the MAGA hat as a crimson ritual crown, drenched in the sacred sweat of empire. But now, now, we have a second coming. We have Trumpism 2.0, and it is a revolution beyond revolutions — a final reckoning that promises to devour the remains of the corrupted system and rebuild something ancient, something powerful, something terrifying in its purity.

The liberal globalist order is a cheap whore's perfume, thick, suffocating, manufactured in the toxic laboratories of Davos, sold at IMF bazaars, sprayed on corpses in Gaza and Ukraine, the smell of death masquerading as progress. It was an illusion, a manufactured mirage carefully marketed to the gullible masses, a grand theater of power where the actors changed but the script remained the same. Alexander Dugin smelled it first, called it by its name: Kali Yuga, the dark age, the tyranny of the Merchant, the ascendancy of Mammon. The priests of liberalism had chanted their mantras of progress and equality while they bled nations dry, crushed the spirit of civilizations, and bound entire populations in the invisible chains of financial slavery. *Esoteric Trumpism* charted the metaphysics of its destruction, but *The Trump Revolution* — Dugin's own revelatory reckoning — drives a tank through its heart. This is not theory. This is practice. This is steel and fire, elections and assassinations, coups and counter-coups. This is the shattered empire lashing out blindly, caught off guard by the forces it once sought to control. The words are weapons. The book is a battlefield.

Trump is a revenant, the ghost of Andrew Jackson, Teddy Roosevelt, and the cosmic bull of Mithras. He is the American god of war, incarnated in flesh and blood, wielding a smartphone in one hand and the thunderbolt of Zeus in the other. *Esoteric Trumpism* knew this. It told us of his archetypal presence, the Orange Emperor who defied the cosmic Lovecraftian financiers. But here, in *The Trump Revolution*, we are beyond myth, beyond prophecy. This is the raw data of war: geopolitics written in the blood of the Deep State's vanquished pawns, the trans-Pacific battles for supremacy, the annihilation of NATO's dogma, and the secret meetings where Marco Rubio's lips tremble as he is told that history is no longer in his hands and that multipolarity is here to stay. This is the moment when the puppets realize the strings have been cut, when the handlers find themselves powerless, when the enforcers of the old order stand exposed as frauds. The Great Powers have returned. The Atlanticists are drowning in their own obsolescence, their grip slipping from the levers of control they once held with arrogant certainty.

But what is power? Who holds it? The technocrats in Silicon Valley now kneel at the altar of Musk, a formidable Faustian figure reshaping the technological and political landscape and opening up the glorious road towards an Archeofuturist horizon. Musk is neither entirely with the technocrats nor entirely against them. He is a force of chaos, an agent of acceleration, a visionary who builds rockets to escape Earth while planting his flag in the heart of America's fractured consciousness. In *Esoteric Trumpism*, the conflict was spiritual — a battle between the Logos and the rot of postmodernity. Now, Dugin shows us the practical implications: technology as the final field of battle, the algorithm as the new assassin, the digital coup d'état that will render the old regimes obsolete. Trump, the cyber-Kaiser, the AI-MAGA commander, merging with the machine but keeping his soul intact. The singularity will wear a red tie. The battlefield is no longer confined to geography. It stretches across the digital plains, fought not with bullets but with information, with narrative control, with the power to define reality itself. The war is already being waged, and those who cannot adapt will be left as footnotes in history.

The book pulsates with the energy of acceleration — not the sterile acceleration of Silicon Valley demons but the fire of multipolarity. What *Esoteric Trumpism* grasped in parable, *The Trump Revolution* lays out in strategy: Russia and China as the dual Heartland forces, the new Rome and Byzantium of a post-liberal world. The maps are being redrawn, not with pens, but with the movement of armies, the collapse of markets, the shifting sands of loyalty. No longer is America the imperial master; instead, Trump wields power like a Roman general, retreating to consolidate, forging new pacts, preparing for the final battle against the suicidal bureaucrats of Brussels and Washington. The West has become a paper tiger, its illusions of strength shattered by its own decadence, its armies filled with weak men and demoralized mercenaries. But Trump, in his reckless and defiant glory, does not seek to salvage the West as it is. He seeks to forge something new, something harder, something that remembers what it means to conquer.

And yet, the enemy remains. The enemy who has always been there. The enemy with its thousands of masks. The eldritch overseers of unfathomable financial dominion, the abyssal architects of a soulless woke horror labyrinth. BlackRock as the vulture feeding off the carcasses of nations. Dugin is merciless. In *The Trump Revolution*, he does not theorize their destruction; he documents its inevitability. They are no longer gods. They are no longer even men. They are insects under the boot of the new world order. Not their order. *Ours.* The war is not yet over, but the tide has turned. The illusion is breaking. The narratives are collapsing. The people are waking up.

There is no return to normal. No return to the old America, the America of Reaganite fantasies and neoliberal wet dreams. Trump has gone too far. The empire has cracked. *Esoteric Trumpism* was the prophecy. *The Trump Revolution* is the execution. It does not speak of possibilities. It speaks of inevitabilities. The Great Powers are rising. The Globalist Cathedral is in ruins. The Swamp has been burned, and from its ashes rises something ancient, something terrible, something divine. This is the Trumpian *Ragnarök*. This is history breaking apart and reassembling itself in a new form.

Welcome to the Renewed World Order. It is not for the weak.

Dresden, Germany—27 February 2025

INTRODUCTION

N THIS SHORT BOOK, I have gathered fresh material on the fundamental events that took place in the United States during Donald
Trump's election to the presidency. Trump's first term was already
extraordinary, disrupting the monotonous process of liberal globalization that had essentially begun in the West immediately after World
War Two (or even earlier, with World War One and Woodrow Wilson's
Fourteen Points, which declared the U.S. as the guarantor and driver of
global liberal democracy). This process culminated in the dissolution
of the Warsaw Pact and the collapse of the Soviet Union in 1991. While
Trump's first term could still be interpreted as a temporary disruption,
his second term, along with the circumstances of his triumphant election, constitutes a true revolution — a Conservative Revolution, if you
will — as his opponents were the liberals who had appropriated the
label of "progressives."

Already during the era of Trump 1.0, it became clear that the global
balance of power and the configuration of dominant ideologies were
shifting irreversibly. It was then that I first proposed revising the fundamental law of classical geopolitics, which posits the confrontation
of only two global civilizations — Land and Sea — and introduced the
theory of a distributed Heartland to describe the newly emerging multipolar world. It was Trump who led me to the idea that the opposition
between Sea and Land, as two vectors of civilizational development
on which classical geopolitics is based, was no longer strictly planetary but had instead shifted within each of the major civilizations.
The electoral map of the United States reinforced this realization: the

inland states voted for Trump, while both the West and East Coasts remained loyal to the Democrats and supported Trump's opponent, Hillary Clinton. This time, the primary opposition was not between America and Eurasia but within America itself. Trump embodied the conservative Heartland within the U.S. context — the core of the civilization of the Land — while the progressive coasts, aligned with liberalism, chose globalism and the civilization of the Sea. Geopolitics had become regional rather than global.

Under the conditions of emerging multipolarity, the coastal regions (the Rimland of classical geopolitics) asserted their autonomy. China's Heartland, with the Communist Party and Xi Jinping in a leading role, was clearly defined, while the coasts remained more entangled in globalism and the world capitalist system. In India, another civilization state, the Land found its expression in the conservative politics of Narendra Modi, while the globalist-backed (particularly by Soros networks) Rahul Gandhi became the symbol of the Sea. But it all began with U.S. electoral geopolitics and the Trump 1.0 phenomenon. Trump's second coming into major politics and the final maturation of his ideology, Trumpism, took place between his first and second presidencies. Trumpism has emerged as a unique phenomenon, combining the long-marginalized national-populist agenda of paleoconservatives with an unexpected shift in Silicon Valley, where influential high-tech tycoons have begun aligning with conservative politics. The most surprising development has been the rapid shift of high-tech tycoons towards Trump's conservative camp. The icon of this great transition has been none other than the world's richest man, entrepreneur, and investor, Elon Musk, who has added a fundamentally new dimension to Trumpism. Thus, Trump's second term has become the final chord in the geopolitics of a multipolar world, marking the overturning of the entire liberal-globalist ideology.

Observing the early steps of Trumpism — from the debates with Biden and Kamala Harris, to the assassination attempts, the campaign, and the deafening election victory, to the inauguration and the first actions of the new administration in the White House — prompted me to write a series of essays and take part in programmatic interviews. In them, I sought to analyze the mind-boggling and unexpected processes unfolding in the United States, as well as to trace their impact on the most volatile zone of world politics: the Middle East.

The result is this book, which abruptly stops halfway through precisely because Trumpism is advancing daily, with each new step deserving no less attention than what came before. However, I have chosen to focus on the events of the first half of February 2025, as the main trends have already emerged with clarity. Naturally, we must continue to observe the unfolding Conservative Revolution under Trump. But that will be the subject of the next book.

We chose the subtitle *A New Order of Great Powers* to capture in a single phrase the new world order that has replaced defeated and trampled liberal globalism.

The American Democrat and globalist Michael McFaul, with whom I have engaged in repeated debates, both in person and on social media, posed a rather desperate question after the first salvos of Trumpism:

"How can a liberal internationalist (i.e., a globalist like himself) survive under Trump's illiberal nationalism?"

The core of the question is well-formulated: the liberal internationalism of the globalist elites has been challenged and radicalized by the illiberal nationalism of Trumpism.

This "illiberal nationalism" has become the ideological axis of the MAGA (Make America Great Again) movement. The United States is no longer presented as the global distributor of liberal democracy and its guarantor on a planetary scale. Instead, it is redefined as a Great Power — focused on its own greatness, sovereignty, and prosperity.

To all other nations, America now simply wishes them well, but abdicates responsibility for their fate.

Liberalism — overthrown within the U.S. itself and increasingly discredited abroad — along with internationalism, has been abolished, replaced by the principle of "America First." Moving forward, the United States will recognize only other Great Powers — which, in Trump's view, include Russia, China, and India. All other nations are free to act as they see fit — whether by seeking patrons or establishing new Great Powers based on civilizational identity.

At its core, this is multipolarity — but not the humane and cooperative multipolarity envisioned by Russia, China, and alliances such as BRICS. Instead, it is a colder, more cynical, and harsher version of multipolarity. The Order of Great Powers is how the Trumpists themselves define multipolarity. And significantly, the new U.S. Secretary of State, Marco Rubio, has explicitly acknowledged that the world is now multipolar. However, there are important nuances in how the United States and other civilization states interpret multipolarity. This book explores these themes through a collection of essays, articles, reports, and interviews.

PART 1

DECOUPLING

INTERNATIONAL
UNCERTAINTY 2025

Speech at the conference "International Uncertainty 2025" at the Moscow State Institute of International Relations, December 2024.

I N THE MODERN WORLD ORDER, there are several levels of uncertainty (indetermination):

1) The Uncertainty of the Phase Transition from Unipolarity to Multipolarity

- It is impossible to say definitively whether we are already in a multipolar world or still in a unipolar one. Heidegger's *noch nicht* ("not yet") remains an acute philosophical problem.

- Multipolarity is on the rise, while unipolarity is in decline, but its agony could prove fatal. The latest desperate — sometimes successful — attacks by globalists against Russia (in Ukraine, Georgia, Moldova, Romania, and Syria) show that unipolarity cannot yet be written off. The dragon of globalism is mortally wounded but still alive.

- In the field of international relations, bipolarity was conceptualized by Kenneth Waltz. Even after the collapse of the Soviet Union, he saw China as the second pole. Unipolarity was formulated by Robert Gilpin. Multipolarity has been outlined by Samuel Huntington and Fabio Petito.

2) The Uncertainty in the Theoretical Definition of Multipolarity

What exactly constitutes a "pole"? Is it a sovereign state, as in the Westphalian system and classical realism? Or is it a civilization? If so, what is the political status of such a cultural-religious concept?

The best answer has been provided by the Chinese scholar of international relations, Zhang Weiwei, who introduced the concept of the civilization state. Russian President Vladimir Putin and Foreign Minister Sergey Lavrov use this term frequently. A civilization state is a civilization (with a well-developed system of traditional values and a strong identity) that is organized as a super-state, attracting constellations of nations and states that share a common civilizational paradigm.

However, today, the term "pole" or "center" (in the case of polycentrism) is understood in different ways: some refer to independent large states, others to civilizations (politically unintegrated), and still others to fully realized civilization states.

As of now, there are four fully formed civilization states:

- The collective West ("NATO-land")
- Russia
- China
- India.

However, there are more civilizations. To the four listed above, we must add the Islamic, African, and Latin American civilizations, which have yet to integrate into super-state formats.

Additionally, the West may split into North America and Europe. A Buddhist civilization is also a potential development.

Alongside this conceptual uncertainty and the open-ended process of civilizations and states transforming into civilization states, another critical issue arises: *frontiers*. This is a fundamental element in the development of a Theory of a Multipolar World. A frontier is a zone where two or more civilizations overlap, with or without the presence of small sovereign states. Frontiers belong to the second uncertainty category.

3) The Uncertainty of Trump and His Strategy

Trump is unlikely to accept multipolarity — he is an advocate of American hegemony. However, he envisions it radically differently from the globalists who have dominated U.S. policy for the past several decades (regardless of whether they were Democrats or Republicans).

Globalists equate military-political dominance, economic superiority, and a liberal ideology that enforces anti-traditional values worldwide (including within the U.S. itself). In this view, hegemony is not the hegemony of a country but of an international ideological liberal system.

Trump, in contrast, believes that national interests should come first, supported by traditional American values. In other words, his approach represents *right-conservative hegemony*, ideologically opposed to the *left-liberal hegemony* of Clinton, Bush Jr. (neocon), Obama, and Biden.

What Trumpism will ultimately mean for international relations remains uncertain. It could objectively accelerate the emergence of multipolarity or, conversely, slow it down.

In 2025, we will be dealing with all three forms of uncertainty simultaneously. It is thus necessary to elevate the term *uncertainty* to the status of an independent and multifaceted concept — one that is crucial for accurately understanding global processes.

DECOUPLING DEFINED

I N THE COMING DECADES, the term that will undoubtedly dominate discussions is *decoupling*. The English word "decoupling" literally means "disconnecting a pair" and can be applied to a wide range of phenomena — from physics to economics. In all cases, it refers to the breaking of a link between two systems that, to some degree, depend on each other.

There is no exact equivalent for this term in Russian, though "disconnection," "separation," or "breaking the link" capture its essence. The Chinese term 脱鈎 (*tuōgōu*), meaning "to separate" (脱) and "hook" (鈎), is also relevant. Nevertheless, it is preferable to retain the English term *decoupling* in Russian, and here is why.

In a broad sense, at the level of global civilizational processes, *decoupling* is the direct opposite of *globalization*. The term "globalization" (of Latin origin but widely used in English) refers to the interconnection of all states and cultures according to rules and algorithms established by the West.

To "be global" means to be like the modern West — to adopt its cultural values, economic mechanisms, technological solutions, political institutions and protocols, information systems, aesthetic preferences, and ethical criteria as something universal, total, obligatory, and nonnegotiable. In practice, this means linking non-Western societies to the West and to each other in such a way that Western rules and norms dictate the framework. In this unipolar globalization, there is one main center — the West — and then all others. As Samuel Huntington put it: "*The West and the rest.*" The "rest" were meant to integrate with the

West, thereby ensuring a single planetary global system — a postmodern empire with its metropolis at the center of humanity, namely, the Western world.

Participation in globalization and recognition of supranational institutions (such as the WTO, WHO, IMF, World Bank, ICC, ECHR, and ultimately, the emerging World Government, represented in embryonic form by the Trilateral Commission or the Davos Forum) was an act of systemic integration, expressed by another term: *coupling*. Between the collective West and any other country, culture, or civilization, a hierarchical relationship was established — leader and follower. The West functioned as the *master*, while the non-West was the *slave*. Along this *coupling* axis, the entire system of global politics, economy, information, technology, industry, finance, and resources was structured.

In this framework, the West represented the *future* — "progress," "development," "evolution," "reforms." The rest of the world was expected to integrate into the West and follow it under the logic of "catch-up development."

Globalists divided the world into three zones:

1) The "rich North" (essentially the West — USA, EU, Australia, Japan)

2) The "semi-periphery" (primarily the more developed BRICS countries)

3) The "poor South" (everyone else).

China entered globalization in the early 1980s under Deng Xiaoping. Russia joined on far less favorable terms in the early 1990s under Yeltsin. Gorbachev's reforms were also aimed at "coupling" with the West ("the common European home"). India followed later. Each country was "hooked" into globalization, meaning integration into the Western-centric world order.

THE PROCESSES OF GLOBALIZATION AND THE EMERGENCE OF DECOUPLING

THE PROCESSES OF globalization accelerated from the late 1980s but began to stall and slow down in the 2000s. The most significant factor in this reversal of globalization's trajectory was Putin's policy. Initially, he sought to integrate Russia into globalization (e.g., through WTO accession), but he simultaneously insisted on sovereignty — directly contradicting the core principle of the globalists: the drive toward de-sovereignization, de-nationalization, and the prospect of establishing a World Government. Putin quickly distanced himself from the IMF and the World Bank, rightly observing that these institutions used "coupling" to serve Western interests, often directly against Russia.

Simultaneously, China, which had derived maximum benefit from globalization by leveraging its involvement in the global economy, financial system, and especially the relocation of Western industries to Southeast Asia (where labor costs were significantly lower), also reached the limits of this strategy's advantages. However, China had always maintained sovereignty in certain areas — rejecting Western-controlled liberal democracy (as seen in Tiananmen Square) and establishing full national control over the internet and digital sphere. This became particularly evident under Xi Jinping, who openly declared China's course not towards Western-centric globalism but towards its own model of world politics based on multipolarity.

Putin also firmly established Russia's course towards multipolarity, and other semi-periphery countries, particularly BRICS nations, gradually leaned towards this model as well.

Tensions between Russia and the West reached their peak with the start of the Special Military Operation (SMO) in Ukraine, after which the West rapidly severed ties with Moscow — economically (sanctions), politically (an unprecedented wave of Russophobia), in energy (the destruction of the Nord Stream pipelines), technological exchanges (a ban on technology transfers to Russia), and even in sports (a series of arbitrary disqualifications of Russian athletes and bans on participation in the Olympics). In other words, in response to the SMO — Putin's full assertion of Russian sovereignty — the West initiated *decoupling*.

At this point, the term "decoupling" took on its full depth of meaning. It is not merely about breaking ties; it signifies a new operational regime for two systems, each of which must now function independently of the other. For the U.S. and the EU, *decoupling* appears as a punishment for Russia's "misconduct," effectively forcing it out of development processes and mechanisms. For Russia, however, this enforced autarky — mitigated by strengthened and even expanded ties with non-Western countries — represents a decisive step towards restoring full geopolitical sovereignty, which had been significantly undermined and almost entirely lost between the late 1980s and early 1990s.

Who exactly initiated *decoupling*, i.e., Russia's removal from the Western-centric unipolar global structure, is difficult to determine unequivocally. Formally, Russia launched the SMO, but the West had long been pushing and provoking it through its Ukrainian proxy instruments. Regardless, the fact remains: Russia has entered a process of *decoupling* from the West and the globalism it promotes. And this is only the beginning. The next inevitable stages lie ahead.

First and foremost, Russia must undertake a consistent and fundamental rejection of the universal applicability of Western norms — in economics, politics, education, technology, culture, art, information, ethics, and more. *Decoupling* does not simply mean deteriorating or severing relations; it goes much deeper. It entails a reassessment of fundamental civilizational frameworks that had long positioned the West as a model for Russia, with its historical developmental stages seen as an unquestionable blueprint for all other nations and civilizations, including Russia itself. For over two centuries — under the Romanovs, during the Soviet period (despite its critique of capitalism), and especially in the era of liberal reforms from the 1990s until February 2022 — Russia engaged in *coupling*, never fully questioning the universality of the Western developmental path.

Even communists, despite their belief in the necessity of overcoming capitalism, first sought to construct a socialist system that initially relied on capitalist industrialization and development, accepting the "objective necessity" of formation shifts. Even Trotsky and Lenin's vision of a world revolution was, in essence, a *coupling* process — a form of "internationalism" aimed at aligning with the West, albeit to unite the global proletariat and escalate their struggle. Under Stalin, the Soviet Union essentially became a civilization state, but this was achieved by deviating from strict Marxist orthodoxy and relying on its own strengths and the creative genius of its people.

When Stalinism's energy and practice waned, the Soviet Union resumed its drift towards the West in line with *coupling* logic — and consequently collapsed. The liberal reforms of the 1990s represented a renewed push towards *coupling*, marked by Atlanticism and a pro-Western orientation among elites. Even under Putin's early rule, Russia sought to maintain *coupling* at all costs — until the contradiction became irreconcilable between globalization and Putin's determination to reinforce state sovereignty (which proved nearly impossible within the framework of ongoing globalization — neither theoretically nor practically).

Now, Russia has consciously, firmly, and irreversibly embarked on *decoupling*. This is why we have chosen to use the English term itself.

Coupling meant integration into the West, recognition of its structures, values, and technologies as universal standards, and a systematic dependence on it — including the desire to join, catch up with, or emulate it (or, at the very least, substitute imported goods and technologies once cut off). *Decoupling*, on the other hand, signifies a rejection of all these premises, reliance not only on Russia's own strengths but also on its own values, identity, history, and spirit.

Of course, we do not yet fully grasp the depth of this transformation, as Westernization in Russia — and the broader history of *coupling* — has been ongoing for several centuries. Despite intermittent setbacks, the West has persistently penetrated Russian society. Western influence is no longer just external — it is deeply embedded within us. Consequently, *decoupling* will be extremely challenging. It entails complex operations to "purge Western influences from society," an endeavor even more profound than the Soviet-era critique of the bourgeois system. Back then, the debate was framed within the context of two competing models of a singular (Western-originated) civilization — capitalist and socialist. Even socialism was built upon Western concepts of development, theories, metrics, and evaluation criteria.

A century earlier, Russian Slavophiles took a bolder stance, calling for a systemic rejection of Westernization and a return to Russia's own roots. This was, in essence, the first step towards *decoupling*. Unfortunately, this movement, which was quite popular in 19th- and early-20th-century Russia, never fully triumphed. Today, we are compelled to complete what the Slavophiles — and later, Russian Eurasianists — began. We must defeat the West's claim to universality, globalism, and exceptionalism.

In a sense, *decoupling* has been imposed upon Russia by the West. But, perhaps, this reflects a deeper act of Providence. Consider the 2024 Paris Olympics opening ceremony: the West banned Russia from participating, ostensibly as a punishment. Yet, instead of a penalty, it became a form of salvation — rescuing Russia from humiliation. The grotesque spectacle of depravity and the dismal sight of swimmers floundering in polluted waters turned the event into the opposite of what was intended. Thus, in the realm of sports, *decoupling* demonstrated its healing power. By cutting Russia off, the West is, paradoxically, aiding its recovery and revival.

If we now turn our attention to the rest of the world, we will see that Russia is not alone on the path of *decoupling*. All those nations and civilizations that favor a multipolar world order are undergoing the same process.

Recently, in a conversation with a prominent Chinese oligarch and investor, I heard him speak about *decoupling* firsthand. With full confidence, my interlocutor asserted that the *decoupling* between China and the U.S. is inevitable and has already begun. The only question is that the West seeks to implement it on terms favorable to itself, while China is pursuing the opposite — its own advantage. Until recently, China had successfully extracted benefits from globalization, but now the situation demands a reassessment and a reliance on its own model, which China closely associates with the success of Greater Eurasian integration (in partnership with Russia) and the implementation of the Belt and Road Initiative. According to my influential Chinese interlocutor, *decoupling* will define China-West relations for the coming decades.

India is also steadily and decisively embracing multipolarity. While there is no talk yet of full *decoupling* from the West, Prime Minister Narendra Modi recently openly proclaimed a course of decolonizing the Indian mind. This means that in this vast civilization state (Bharat), at least in the realm of ideas — arguably the most important domain — the course has been set for intellectual *decoupling*. Western modes of thought, philosophy, and culture are no longer regarded as absolute models by the new generation of Indians. Moreover, the memory of the horrors of British colonialism and subjugation remains vivid. After all, colonization itself was a form of *coupling*, a process of modernization and Westernization, which is why Karl Marx himself supported it.

It is evident that full-scale *decoupling* is also underway in the Islamic world. A real war is being waged by Palestinians and Shia Muslim groups in the region against the West's proxy in the Middle East: Israel. The stark opposition between modern Western values and Islamic religious and cultural norms has long been a central theme of anti-Western policy in the Muslim world. The grotesque parade of degeneracy at the opening ceremony of the Paris Olympics only added fuel to the fire. Significantly, it was the Islamic Republic of Iran that reacted most strongly to the blasphemous portrayal of Christ in the event's sacrilegious staging. Islam is clearly oriented towards *decoupling*, and this process is irreversible.

Similar developments are unfolding in other civilizations — whether in the renewed wave of decolonization among African nations or in the policies of many Latin American countries. The deeper they engage with multipolarity and align themselves with the BRICS bloc, the more acutely *decoupling* emerges as a pressing issue within their societies.

And finally, we can observe that the desire to withdraw within one's own borders is increasingly manifesting itself in the West as well. Right-wing populists in Europe and Trump supporters in the United States are openly advocating a "Fortress Europe" and a "Fortress America," meaning *decoupling* from non-Western societies — against immigration flows, the erosion of identity, and de-sovereignization. Even under Biden, a staunch globalist and ardent proponent of preserving unipolarity, we saw certain unmistakable moves towards protectionist measures. The West itself is beginning to close off, taking steps towards *decoupling*.

Thus, we began with the assertion that the word "decoupling" will be key in the coming decades. This is evident, but few people yet fully comprehend the depth of this process and the intellectual, philosophical, political, organizational, social, and cultural efforts it will demand from all of humanity — our societies, nations, and peoples. As we detach from the global West, we face the necessity of restoring, reviving, and reaffirming our own values, traditions, cultures, principles, beliefs, customs, and foundations. We are only taking the first steps in this direction. This is a positive development, but the road ahead is arduous and long. We must acknowledge this and consolidate all the creative, spiritual, and physical potential of our societies.

Decoupling is the practical realization of building a multipolar world.

THE NUCLEAR PENDULUM

Excerpt from the debates held in December 2024 between Alexander Dugin and John Mearsheimer, with the participation of former California Governor Jerry Brown.

Moderator's Question: What is your vision of the new multipolar world? We often talk about multipolarity and the balance of power. But it is interesting to hear each participant's perspective. What will happen to the balance of power in a multipolar world? Will every state seek to acquire nuclear weapons? What does this look like in a multipolar world? Will military alliances continue to exist?

Alexander Dugin: First and foremost, it is important to understand what constitutes a pole in a multipolar world. In my view, which differs from classical realism, a pole does not necessarily coincide with a nation-state. A full-fledged pole in a multipolar world system must possess nuclear weapons. It must be a true civilization — with all its cultural, historical, social, political, and economic attributes. A pole is something fundamentally different from a nation-state, even a large one. Not every nation-state possesses nuclear weapons. But a pole must certainly have them.

At present, we already have several poles:

1) The first pole is the West — NATO-land, but the United States itself can also be considered a separate pole. The United States and Western Europe can more or less easily divide into two poles and still remain sovereign, full-fledged poles — especially the U.S.

The two-part Western pole (U.S. and EU) may well split into two distinct poles.

2) China is a pole, and this needs no further argument. It is more than just a country — it is a civilization state.

3) Russia is a pole. And Russia is more than just a state. By all parameters — first and foremost, its geographical scale, nuclear arsenal, as well as historical and political tradition — it qualifies as a pole.

Thus, we currently have three or four existing poles, all of which possess nuclear weapons and represent distinct civilizations.

India is the next pole. India also possesses nuclear weapons and is a unique civilization with an ancient history and a rich geopolitical presence.

Therefore, the issue is not about the proliferation of nuclear weapons. Nuclear capabilities are already in the hands of four or five poles.

If we consider the Islamic pole, we must acknowledge that it is not yet fully formed. It still needs to take shape. However, we already see at least one country — Pakistan — that possesses nuclear weapons. Iran, meanwhile, is in the process of acquiring them. Thus, an Islamic nuclear bomb is already present or on the horizon.

From a civilizational standpoint — religious, historical, and geopolitical — the Islamic world has the potential to become a serious and significant sovereign pole. However, to achieve this, it must overcome many internal contradictions. This process will be objectively driven by Israel's aggressive policies in the Middle East and its increasing assaults on Islamic holy sites in Jerusalem. This issue may be postponed, but it cannot be avoided.

If we analyze the world in terms of poles rather than states, we can also speak of the formation of two additional poles — the African pole and the Latin American pole. Imagine a scenario in which nuclear weapons are transferred to an African power or a coalition of African states — or even to the Pan-African Union. At present, no single

African country has yet claimed leadership in continental integration, but in time, an independent African pole will emerge. It must appear.

The same applies to Latin America. I believe that Brazil is the first country that could aspire to nuclear capabilities because it is far more developed and technologically advanced than other regional states. This is why Brazil represents Latin America in BRICS. Brazil already has its own aircraft industry and even submarines.

In other words, we must acknowledge that nuclear multipolarity is approaching.

It is unrealistic to expect that nuclear weapons will be distributed among all countries. This is neither feasible nor necessary. The multipolar world order is not about nuclear sovereignty for every single nation. It is about something entirely different.

The theory of a multipolar world is still an underdeveloped field in international relations. However, the foundations have already been laid — primarily through my own works, textbooks, articles, and lectures, as well as through official documents from Russia and China and the speeches of many political figures such as Putin, Xi Jinping, Narendra Modi, and others.

The West continues to deny the multipolar world as a new reality. This is something Western strategic thought tries to silence and reject. Globalists and proponents of woke ideology are completely intolerant of anything that does not align with their ideological dogma. In doing so, they are increasingly losing touch with reality. Unfortunately, most strategists do not heed the analyses and ideas of scholars like John Mearsheimer and other objective classical thinkers. The globalist West still operates within outdated paradigms. Globalists perceive multipolarity as a challenge, an affront, something scandalous rather than an objective reality. If they accepted the actual state of affairs, they could rationally and objectively study the multipolar world as a fact, and the issue of nuclear proliferation would appear in a much more realistic context.

Jerry Brown: Let's discuss the Nuclear Non-Proliferation Treaty. Article 6 clearly states that nuclear powers — Russia, the United States, China, and others — are obligated to strive for disarmament and negotiate in good faith. This is based on the reality that nuclear weapons are not under absolute control by the states that possess them. There are technological risks, software vulnerabilities, and human error. False alarms are a real possibility, and in a hostile world, such risks increase. Moreover, as the U.S., Russia, and China develop new nuclear weapons systems and modernize existing arsenals, the world becomes even more dangerous. My question is directed at both speakers, but primarily at Professor Dugin: How does Putin view negotiations on reducing existing nuclear stockpiles? Even if there is no further proliferation, the growing threat of nuclear exchange remains. Who knows how catastrophic that could be? Is there any inclination in Russia or in Putin's thinking towards a significant reduction of nuclear arms? The same applies to the U.S., which has launched a modernization program, and to China, which is currently in the process of building an additional 1,000 nuclear warheads. Where does Russia stand concerning Article 6 and the question of whether to increase or reduce its nuclear arsenal?

Alexander Dugin: Unfortunately, this is not my area of professional expertise. However, as far as I understand the situation, Russia today is not as concerned with the threat of nuclear proliferation as such but rather with the hegemonic behavior of the U.S., the collective West, and, above all, liberal globalists. Therefore, Russia now faces the possibility of nuclear conflict with the West. The threat of proliferation — such as Iran acquiring nuclear weapons or North Korea advancing its nuclear program — is currently seen as far less of a concern than the risk of direct nuclear confrontation with the West or the possibility of NATO supplying nuclear weapons to Ukraine.

At present, all issues related to nuclear proliferation among Russia's allies are secondary. That is why I believe it is not particularly important for Russia to limit Iran's nuclear development or to prevent advancements in nuclear technology by North Korea or Pakistan. Strategically, this is not a priority, as Russia perceives itself to be on the brink of nuclear war with the West.

The current nuclear balance between Russia and NATO is far more crucial than the issue of proliferation itself. In order to deter or counterbalance this Western threat, I believe Russia could take several unconventional steps — not only in developing new weapons and improving delivery systems but also in matters of proliferation.

We are in a unique historical moment. Russia believes it has been attacked by the West. We see ourselves at war with a nuclear-armed West. This is a fundamentally different period in history. If we were to envision a return to a peaceful tripolar system, where mutual understanding and balance of power were maintained without direct military conflict, then perhaps the idea of restricting nuclear proliferation would seem rational. But not now.

PUTIN AS THE ARCHITECT
OF A NEW ORDER

V LADIMIR PUTIN'S SPEECH at the Valdai Club on November 7, 2024, has already become historic without exaggeration. Churchill's Fulton speech once marked the beginning of the Cold War, entering history as a moment when a world leader outlined the future of humanity — a future of conflict, intense competition, and ideological struggle. But today, our president has described a completely different future: the architecture of a new world order, or as he himself put it, a new *cosmos*, which humanity itself must create, listing its fundamental principles.

Firstly, this new order is based on *justice*, respect for the cultures of all peoples, and *true* — not superficial — *democracy*. As Putin stated, democracy is the power of the majority, not the way modern globalists and liberals define it — as the rule of minorities. True democracy is the power of nations that choose their own historical path, and no one has the right to take that sovereign choice away from them.

Secondly, the foundation of this new world order consists of *traditional values*. A world cannot be built upon the principles that, until recently, U.S. leaders insisted upon — leaders who, thankfully, were defeated in the last election. These figures sought to erase human nature itself — to eliminate gender, to abolish the family, to replace human beings with post-human, transhumanist entities.

And this is not some dystopian fantasy; it is precisely what the globalist elites of the contemporary collective West have been steering humanity towards. It is against this unipolar world order, founded on

Western liberal hegemony, that President Putin has delivered a decisive "no."

Not long ago, when Putin spoke of multipolarity, many assumed these were mere words, meant only to justify Russia's opposition to the West. But in reality, it is something far greater. It is a *strategy rooted in traditional values and respect for the diversity of all cultures and civilizations* — not just one civilization declaring itself "progressive" and, on that basis, imposing its principles on the entire world.

Furthermore, this is a *historic speech by a leader not only of Russia but of the entire world and humanity as a whole.* Putin's emphasis on the fact that Western neoliberalism has degenerated into a totalitarian ideology is of paramount importance. He also pointed out that the West itself is not our true adversary; our real enemy is the *globalist elite* — fanatical, intolerant, and determined to impose inconceivable rules upon humanity.

This speech, clearly not a spontaneous one but carefully prepared, has already been confirmed in practice: by the *triumphant BRICS summit in Kazan* and by *Trump's victory in the U.S. presidential election.* The world has chosen traditional values over globalist dictatorship. Americans themselves have rejected the neoliberal clique, telling them in no uncertain terms: "Get out!"

Against this backdrop, our President's Valdai speech appears *prophetic.* And more than that — Putin does not merely speak; he acts. A significant portion of his vision has already been realized, and the rest will undoubtedly follow.

In his speech, the head of the Russian state also emphasized that the globalists (specifically the globalists, not just the West — we need to relearn how to distinguish these concepts, as Trump's America is not the same as Biden's, Obama's, Bush's, Clinton's, or Soros' America) wanted to defeat Russia, to break it, but they failed. Inflicting a strategic defeat on Russia has not been achieved and will never be achieved by anyone, ever.

And finally, over the past decades, we have already demonstrated to the world our ability to defend our ideals, values, traditional way of life, and our rejection of the agenda imposed on us by liberal globalist elites.

However, in the difficult situations of previous years, when we were not yet on the offensive and could not prove our ability to resist the pressure of NATO, globalist regimes, and their satraps so persistently and effectively, these same thoughts, which Vladimir Putin expressed clearly and directly today, were articulated with slightly different nuances.

Now a new strength is behind us: in the Special Military Operation, Russia has hardened, become much stronger and more resolute. We have finally developed our Russian state idea, an idea rooted in Orthodox and all traditional religions, as well as the indigenous peoples of our country, for whom Russia is the only homeland. And because of this, we have already become a hundred times stronger.

When we finally liberate Ukraine, we will become a thousand times stronger. And then, having endured incredible trials, we will prove that we were right at every stage of our journey towards revival. To the return of our role in the global movement of humanity towards a more just, humane, honest, and existentially adequate world.

PART 2

DONALD TRUMP'S CONSERVATIVE REVOLUTION

THE WORLD ON THE EDGE

Biden and Trump: Games of the Apocalypse

This article was written in June 2024, when Biden was officially nominated as the Democratic Party's candidate for President of the United States.

T HE UPCOMING U.S. presidential election, scheduled for November 5, 2024, carries absolute significance. The outcome will not only determine the fate of the United States and even the entire West but also the fate of all humanity. The world is teetering on the brink of nuclear war — a full-scale, total Third World War between Russia and NATO countries. The person who takes the helm of the White House for the next term will ultimately decide whether humanity will continue to exist.

That is why it is crucial to once again examine the two candidates, analyze their platforms, and understand their positions.

Joe Biden and the Ideology of Globalism

Biden is undoubtedly a senile invalid, exhibiting clear signs of advanced dementia. Strangely enough, however, this hardly matters. Biden is merely a facade, a figurehead for the firmly entrenched political elites of the Democratic Party, who have reached a strong consensus around him. In principle, Biden could rule even as a corpse — much like the exhumed dead bodies in annual rituals on the Indonesian island of

Sulawesi during the Ma'nene festival or similar traditions among the Malagasy people of Madagascar. It would change nothing.

Behind him stands a united group of globalists (sometimes referred to as the "World Government" or "the ruling strata"), encompassing not only much of the American Deep State but also the liberal elites of Europe and the world at large.

Ideologically, Biden represents *globalism*, a project aimed at uniting humanity under the rule of liberal technocratic elites by abolishing sovereign nation-states and fully merging different peoples and faiths. This is a kind of modern-day Tower of Babel. Orthodox Christians and many traditionalist Christians of other denominations logically see this as the *arrival of the Antichrist*. Globalists — figures like Yuval Harari, Klaus Schwab, Raymond Kurzweil, and Maurice Strong — openly advocate replacing humanity with artificial intelligence and cyborgs. The abolition of gender and ethnicity has already become a reality in Western societies.

However, Biden himself plays no direct role in executing this project. He does not make decisions; he merely serves as the authorized representative of the international headquarters of globalism.

The Democratic Party's Consensus

Politically, Biden relies on the Democratic Party, which, despite its internal diversity and the presence of non-globalist figures — such as the far-left Bernie Sanders or Robert Kennedy — has reached an internal agreement to support him. Biden's incapacity does not frighten anyone, as real power lies with entirely different, younger, and more rational figures. But the key point is this: Biden is backed by an *ideology that has gained near-universal dominance worldwide*. Liberalism, in various degrees, has permeated global politics and economic elites. It has deeply embedded itself in education, science, culture, information, economics, business, politics, and even technology on a planetary level.

Biden is simply the *convergence point* of this global web. The *Democratic Party of the United States is its political embodiment.* Democrats are increasingly *disregarding the American people themselves*, instead prioritizing global dominance at any cost — even at the cost of World War Three with Russia and China. In a way, they are willing to *sacrifice the United States itself.* This makes them extraordinarily dangerous.

The *neoconservative factions within the U.S.* align with the *globalist agenda* behind Biden. These are former Trotskyists who despise Russia and believe that world revolution is possible only after capitalism's complete triumph — meaning the global West's victory on a worldwide scale. Thus, they have postponed their revolutionary ambitions until capitalist globalization is completed, hoping to return to the idea of proletarian revolution after the liberal West secures global victory.

Neocons act as *hawks*, insist on a *unipolar world*, and fully support *Israel and its genocide in Gaza.* While some neocons exist within the Democratic Party, the majority reside in the Republican Party, forming a faction directly opposed to Trump. In some ways, they act as a *fifth column* within the GOP, serving the interests of Biden and the Democrats.

Support from the Deep State

Finally, there is the *American Deep State* — the extralegal ruling elite of government officials, top bureaucrats, and key figures in the military and intelligence communities. These figures serve as the *"guardians" of American statehood.*

Historically, the Deep State has maintained *two strategic vectors* that align with the traditional political policies of Democrats and Republicans:

1) *Global dominance and the expansion of liberalism* on a planetary scale (Democratic Party strategy)

2) *Strengthening the U.S. as a great superpower* and maintaining its role as the primary hegemon in global politics (Republican Party strategy).

These are not mutually exclusive strategies. Rather, they are two *complementary* approaches leading to the same ultimate goal. The Deep State *preserves* this overarching direction, allowing the electoral process to alternate between these two options. Both fundamentally align with its agenda.

This consensus was most evident when neoconservatives dominated the Republican Party — as seen during George W. Bush's presidency. At that time, globalism essentially merged with *right-wing Atlanticism and hegemony*, forming a united front for a *unipolar world order*. Globalization is inherently unipolar, which is why there was little difference between the foreign policies of Democratic globalists like Clinton and Obama and neoconservative Republicans like George W. Bush.

Today, the Deep State continues to support this line. However, Biden's faction more accurately reflects the interests and values of the *uppermost layers of the American bureaucracy.*

Biden: The Name of War

Biden embodies a *critical mass of power factors* — from ideology to Deep State backing. He also enjoys support from *major financial corporations, global media, and international monopolies.* His personal weakness and cognitive decline compel the globalists behind him to accelerate their undemocratic methods of maintaining power.

At a recent campaign rally, Biden *openly stated*: "It is time to put freedom above democracy." This was not a slip of the tongue — it was the globalist plan. If power cannot be maintained *democratically*, then under the banner of "freedom," any *undemocratic process* can be justified — including, essentially, the establishment of a *globalist dictatorship.*

A war with Russia would provide the legal pretext for such measures. Biden could replicate Zelensky's trick of canceling elections to stay in power. The same Macron could do in France after his crushing defeat by right-wing parties in the European elections, and even Scholz in Germany, who is rapidly losing support.

Globalists in the West are *clearly considering scenarios for direct dictatorship and the abolition of democracy.*

For humanity, Biden's victory — or even his retention of power in any form — would be a catastrophe. The globalists will continue building their *New Babylon*, clinging to the World Government, which will lead to new conflicts and escalations.

Biden means war — *war without end.*

TRUMP AND TRUMPISM

DONALD TRUMP is backed by entirely different forces. He is truly an alternative to Biden and his globalist faction, and this contrast is far sharper than the usual shifts between Democrats and Republicans in the sequence of Clinton — George W. Bush — Obama. This is why Trump's first presidential term was marked by continuous scandal. The American establishment categorically refused to accept him and did not rest until they replaced him with Biden.

Unlike Biden, Trump is a vibrant, unique, impulsive, and strong-willed personality. Despite his age, he remains in good shape — passionate, energetic, and vigorous. Furthermore, while Biden is a team player and essentially a puppet of globalist circles, Trump is a lone figure, the embodiment of the American dream of personal success. He is a narcissist and an egotist but also a highly skilled and successful politician.

Let's examine him more closely.

Trump's Ideological Foundation

Ideologically, Trump draws from classical American conservatives (not neoconservatives!). They are often referred to as *paleoconservatives*. These thinkers uphold the *traditional Republican isolationist tradition*, embodied in Trump's slogan "America First!" One of the most prominent ideological figures in this movement is political philosopher and politician Patrick J. Buchanan, while Steve Bannon, one of the main figures behind the Tea Party movement, at one point championed these ideas within Trump's circle.

These classical conservatives defend traditional values — a family consisting of a man and a woman, the Christian faith, and the preservation of norms and decorum rooted in American culture. In foreign policy, paleoconservatism prioritizes strengthening the U.S. as a sovereign nation-state (hence the slogan "Make America great again") and rejects interventionism in other countries unless there is a direct threat to U.S. security and interests.

From an ideological standpoint, Trump's platform is *entirely opposed to Biden's*. This is why Trump referred to his globalist adversaries with the derisive term *the Swamp*.

Today, this ideology is most commonly associated with Trump himself and is known as *Trumpism*.

Trump's Popular Base

From an electoral and sociological perspective, a significant portion of Americans — especially in the central states (flyover country) between the two coasts — share this ideology. The average American is *conservative and traditionalist*, although the culture of individualism makes many indifferent to the opinions of others, including the government. Their faith in self-reliance fosters skepticism towards the federal government, which is inherently seen as limiting their freedoms.

Trump's ability to directly address this common American — bypassing political, financial, and media elites — enabled him to win the 2016 election.

Paleoconservatives vs. Republican Pragmatists

Since the Republican Party includes both paleoconservatives and neoconservatives, it remains deeply divided. The neocons are closer to Biden and his backers, while Trump's ideology runs directly counter to their core principles. The only common ground is their shared declaration of America's greatness and their commitment to strengthening U.S. military and economic power.

However, *former Trotskyists within the neoconservative movement* have spent decades embedding themselves in U.S. policy circles, establishing influential think tanks and infiltrating existing institutions. Paleoconservatives, by contrast, have lost most of their intellectual infrastructure.

In the 1990s, Buchanan lamented that the *neocons had hijacked the Republican Party*, pushing traditionally oriented politicians to the margins. This presents a structural challenge for Trump.

Neocon Sabotage

During his first term, Trump was forced to rely on some neocons, appointing the hawkish and aggressive John Bolton as his National Security Advisor. Bolton actively undermined Trump's policies and eventually betrayed him outright.

However, elections are critical for the Republican Party, and many high-profile politicians — congressmen, senators, and governors — recognize Trump's immense popularity among the electorate. Even out of pragmatism, they are compelled to support him. This explains Trump's dominant influence among GOP presidential candidates.

For Republicans — not only paleoconservatives but also practical-minded politicians — Trump *holds the key to power.*

Nonetheless, the neocons remain extremely influential, and Trump is unlikely to risk severing ties with them entirely.

Cold Relations with the Deep State

The Deep State's attitude towards Trump has been lukewarm from the start. To the upper echelons of the bureaucracy, Trump appeared to be an upstart and an outsider, relying on ideas that, while popular among ordinary Americans, were seen as dangerous to the establishment. Additionally, he lacked sufficient backing within elite circles.

This explains the immediate conflict with the CIA and other intelligence agencies from the very beginning of Trump's presidency in 2017.

The Deep State is not on Trump's side**. However, it cannot ignore his popularity or the fact that strengthening the U.S. *as a state* does not inherently contradict its long-term interests.

If Trump had the will, he could build a substantial base of support within these circles, but his political temperament does not lend itself to such maneuvering. He prefers to act spontaneously and impulsively, relying on his own strength. This is precisely what endears him to voters, who see him as a familiar American archetype.

A Second Term and Deep State Adaptation

If Trump wins the 2024 election, relations with the Deep State will inevitably shift. Once his enduring political relevance is acknowledged, the Deep State will attempt to establish systemic ties with him.

To Be or Not to Be

The globalists behind Biden will do everything possible to remove Trump from the race and prevent him from returning to the presidency *at any cost*. This could involve *any method*:

- Assassination
- Imprisonment
- Organizing riots and protests
- Attempting a coup or even a civil war.

Alternatively, Biden could *launch World War Three before the end of his term* — a scenario that is far from unlikely.

Given the Deep State's alignment with globalists, any of these options could be pursued.

However, if Trump wins and becomes president again, it will *dramatically reshape global politics*.

First and foremost, a second Trump term would confirm that his first presidency was no accident. It would prove that his victory was not a "regrettable" (for globalists) anomaly, but part of a larger shift.

A *unipolar world and the globalist project* would be rejected not only by multipolar powers — Russia, China, and Islamic nations — but also by the *American people themselves.*

This would deal a devastating blow to the entire liberal-globalist elite. And this time, they might not recover.

Objectively, Trump could become the catalyst for a multipolar world order, in which the U.S. would still play an important role but not a dominant one.

In this new world, "America will be great again" — not as a globalist hegemon but as a sovereign nation-state**.

The Difference Between Biden and Trump

Even with a Trump victory, the conflicts initiated by the globalists will not automatically cease. Trump's demands on Russia to end the war in Ukraine will be realistic but firm. His support for Israel in Gaza and beyond will be just as unconditional as Biden's. Moreover, Trump views Netanyahu as a kindred political spirit. Regarding China, he will pursue a hardline policy, especially increasing pressure on Chinese businesses operating in the U.S.

The main difference between Trump and Biden lies in their approach to foreign policy. Trump will act based on rational calculations of U.S. national interests (consistent with the *realist school* in international relations) and will pragmatically balance power and resources. In contrast, the ideology of Biden's globalist backers is *totalitarian and uncompromising.* Those who refuse to submit to the World Government and surrender their sovereignty will face sanctions and even direct intervention. This aligns with the liberal approach in international relations.

For Trump, nuclear apocalypse is an unacceptable cost for any political goal. For Biden — and more importantly, for those who imagine themselves as the rulers of the *New Babylon* — everything is at stake. Their behavior in a critical situation is unpredictable. Trump, on the other hand, is simply a tough and audacious player — but one restrained by rationality and the pursuit of tangible benefits. Trump is hard to persuade but possible to negotiate with. Biden and his handlers, however, are *irrational*.

The 2024 U.S. election will answer a fundamental question: Does humanity still have a chance, or is it already lost? No more, no less.

WHO RULES AMERICA? THE BEAVIS AND BUTT-HEAD DEBATE

This article was written following the first debate between Biden and Trump, which took place on June 27, 2024.

I N   T H E   1 9 9 0 S, the animated series *Beavis and Butt-Head*, created by Mike Judge, was popular in both the U.S. and Russia. The show's protagonists were two mentally deficient American teenagers, constantly cursing, making absurd statements, and incapable of solving even the simplest everyday problems. Despite their complete incompetence and meaningless existence, they somehow managed to scrape by. Every time a series of idiotic decisions led them to the brink of total disaster, a random fluke or logical inconsistency miraculously saved them — only for them to squander the opportunity immediately, repeating the cycle endlessly. Failure after failure, eating worms, making the worst possible decisions, violating all conceivable logical connections — only to end up watching a heavy metal video, where horned men with guitars ritually devoured women or live goats.

What the world witnessed during the Trump-Biden debates was nothing more than a fresh episode of *Beavis and Butt-Head*. Both candidates eerily resembled the cartoon characters — Trump a remake of Beavis, Biden of Butt-Head. Even Trump's hairstyle matches Beavis' perfectly. The content of the debates was also *straight out of the show*:

Beavis: "You're an old idiot."

Butt-Head: "No, you're an old idiot. I'm only three years older than you, so that means you're almost as old as me. You're almost a hundred."

Beavis: "You're the one pushing a hundred! You're already past it! You talk to ghosts, touch invisible chairs… You've failed at everything, while I've done everything perfectly."

Butt-Head: "No, I did everything perfectly, and you failed at everything. Plus, you're a sleazy womanizer."

Beavis: "I'm not a womanizer! I don't even know who Stormy Daniels is. My lawyers will destroy her."

Butt-Head: "You're going to destroy NATO."

Beavis: "What's NATO?"

Butt-Head: "Why did you even attack the Capitol?"

Beavis: "What's the Capitol? Doesn't matter. You're about to drop dead, and we'll make America great again."

Butt-Head: "I already made America great by letting in lots of little people. You just want to ruin everything. Look at how many migrants have climbed over your wall. They shine in all the colors of the rainbow — I can watch them for hours."

Beavis: "You were scared of a fake rabbit. I'll rebuild my wall and seal all the migrants inside it."

Butt-Head: "I won't let you. I'll send my superhero friend Zelensky after you. He has special *tight pants* that let him fly."

Beavis: "He's a crook — he comes here and robs us. I'll burn him alive with my superpowers."

Butt-Head: "I'll burn you alive, or freeze you solid, for being a sleazy womanizer."

Beavis: "I don't even know who Stormy Daniels is."

And so on.

Meanwhile, all of America watches, *placing bets on which old man will collapse first,* and who will keep spouting nonsense to the end.

Mike Judge's *Beavis and Butt-Head* was a brutal satire of the American adolescent mindset — a superpower that has never matured historically and is entirely unfit to govern humanity. The U.S. is a deranged teenager with a loaded gun. A school shooter nation. And if there's a gun, then — by the logic of an imbecile — it must be fired, at whoever happens to be nearby.

The show's protagonists are teenagers. The debate's participants are elderly men. But that is the *essence of American identity* — America *can never grow up.* It is a *perpetual kidult,* forever stuck between childhood and adulthood.

In psychiatry, there is a condition known as hebephrenia — a mental disorder where an adolescent fails to develop into adulthood, becoming trapped in a perpetual transition phase. Postwar Japan, which *obsessively imitates American culture,* has seen a massive rise in the *hikikomori* phenomenon — young people rejecting adulthood, locking themselves in their rooms, living off their parents, unable to work, marry, or integrate into society. This is a *literal replication of the American cultural pattern.*

Beavis and Butt-Head can never grow up. They are perpetual hebephrenics with a blocked maturation mechanism. This explains the *constant flood of Marvel films,* mass-produced from comic books. These movies are designed for 10–12-year-olds, yet *all of America watches them.* Just like they watch the presidential debates.

Following the debates, the great imbecile superpower declared Beavis-Trump the winner. He held up better, his aggressive hairstyle appeared more convincing, while Sleepy Butt-Head Biden's batteries ran out by the end, reducing him to monotonous wheezing.

If this society, culture, candidates, and electorate are responsible for determining the fate of humanity, then we must acknowledge that *we are doomed.*

It is impossible to reason with or reform a clinically ill adolescent — especially one *with access to nuclear weapons.*

We say that "Russia is governed by God" because its very existence defies explanation. But America, too, has a mystery.

How can a nation with such foundations, such people, and such mental disorders become the world's leading superpower?

This suggests *someone far more serious and invisible* is in control.

And it does *not* appear to be God.

TRUMPISM AS AN IDEOLOGY

The Trump Revolution

RIGHT NOW, people in Russia and around the world are clearly puzzled: what is happening in the United States? President-elect Trump and his closest allies, particularly the dynamic Elon Musk, have launched an almost revolutionary campaign. Trump has yet to take office — this will happen on January 20 — but America and Europe have already begun to shake. This is an ideological and geopolitical tsunami that, to be honest, no one expected. Many assumed that after his election, Trump — much like during his first term — would return to a more or less conventional political course, albeit with his characteristic charisma and spontaneity. It is already clear that this is not the case. Trump is a *revolution*.

That is why this transitional period, as power shifts from Biden to Trump, is the right moment for a serious analysis of what is happening in America. Something *very, very important* is unfolding there.

The Deep State and the History of American Ascendancy

First and foremost, we must clarify: how was Trump elected at all, given the power of the Deep State? This requires a broader examination.

The Deep State in the U.S. represents the core of the government apparatus and the closely linked ideological and economic elites. Government, business, and education in the U.S. form a single interconnected system rather than separate entities. Added to this are traditional American secret societies and elite clubs, which have long served as networking hubs for the ruling class. This entire complex is what is commonly called the "Deep State."

The two main political parties — Democrats and Republicans — are not representatives of fundamentally different ideologies but rather *variations of a single political-economic course*, embodied by the Deep State. Their balance serves only to adjust secondary matters while maintaining public engagement.

After World War Two, the U.S. went through two major phases:

1) The Cold War era (1947–1991), marked by ideological and geopolitical confrontation with the Soviet Union and the socialist bloc

2) The Unipolar World era or the "End of History" (1991–2024), during which the U.S. fully *defeated its opponent* and emerged as the sole political-ideological superpower (or hyperpower).

It was not political parties or individual institutions, but the Deep State that carried forward this unwavering *agenda of global domination*. From the 1990s onward, this dominance became increasingly left-liberal in nature, merging the interests of international capital with progressive individualist culture. This strategy was most fully embraced by the Democratic Party, although neoconservatives within the Republican Party also supported it.

The central assumption behind this strategy was the *belief in continuous, linear growth* — of both the American economy and the world as a whole, alongside the *planetary expansion of liberalism and liberal values*. The assumption was that all nations and societies had accepted the American model — representative democracy, capitalist free markets, individualist cosmopolitan human rights, digital technologies, and Western-centric postmodernist culture. The Deep State fully subscribed to this vision and *served as its enforcer*.

Samuel Huntington's Warning: A Call for Course Correction

As early as the 1990s, some American intellectuals began warning that this approach was flawed in the long term. The clearest expression of this position came from Samuel Huntington, who predicted a "clash of civilizations," the rise of multipolarity, and the crisis of Western-centric globalization.

Instead of pushing for *global liberal homogenization*, Huntington argued for strengthening American identity and uniting other Western societies within a single, regional *Western* civilization — not a *global* one. However, at the time, these warnings were dismissed as excessive caution from several skeptics.

The Deep State fully embraced the optimism of the "End of History," championed by Huntington's main rival, Francis Fukuyama. This explains the *seamless continuity* in U.S. policy under successive presidents — Clinton, Bush, Obama (followed by the "anomaly" of Trump's first presidency), and Biden. Regardless of party affiliation, both Democrats and Republicans (under Bush Jr.) followed the same Deep State globalist strategy — liberalism, unipolarity, and American hegemony.

However, by the early 2000s, this globalist optimism began to falter.

- Russia, under Putin, ceased blindly following the U.S. and began restoring its sovereignty — most notably after Putin's 2007 Munich speech, the 2008 Georgia conflict, the 2014 reunification with Crimea, and especially the 2022 launch of the Special Military Operation. All of these developments *directly contradicted globalist plans*.

- China, especially under Xi Jinping, started pursuing an independent strategy, leveraging globalization for its own benefit while blocking it whenever it threatened national sovereignty.

- The Islamic world witnessed sporadic protests against Western influence — both in the form of political independence movements and cultural resistance to liberal values.

- In India, Prime Minister Narendra Modi led right-wing nationalists and traditionalists to power.

- Anti-colonial sentiments grew in Africa, while Latin American countries increasingly distanced themselves from U.S. influence.

These trends culminated in the formation of BRICS as the embryo of a multipolar international system, largely independent of the West.

Meanwhile, globalist forces, led by Biden's administration and figures like Boris Johnson, Keir Starmer, Emmanuel Macron, and Ursula von der Leyen, sought to intensify their control.

George Soros' ultra-globalist structures became even more aggressive, infiltrating European institutions and launching massive campaigns aimed at destabilizing Modi's government in India, orchestrating new color revolutions in the post-Soviet space (Moldova, Georgia, Armenia), and overthrowing non-aligned regimes in the Islamic world — particularly in Bangladesh and Syria.

But this time, the Deep State's support for the globalists was not unconditional but conditional. Biden and his allies had to pass a test — to prove that nothing serious was happening to globalism and that any issues were merely technical problems that could be resolved through force — whether ideological, media-driven, economic, political, or outright terrorist methods.

The Deep State acted as the judge in this test.**

Biden Loses the Deep State's Trust

But Biden failed. For numerous reasons:

1) Putin's Russia did not surrender and withstood unprecedented pressure — sanctions, confrontation with the Ukrainian terrorist regime backed by all Western nations, economic challenges, a

drastic reduction in natural resource exports, and the severance of ties to high technology. Biden failed to defeat Russia.

2) China did not back down and continued its trade war with the U.S. without suffering critical losses.

3) Modi was not removed during the election campaign.

4) BRICS held a brilliant summit in Kazan, on the soil of Russia, which is at war with the West. Multipolarity continued its rise.

5) Israel, violating all laws and norms, carried out a genocide in Gaza and Lebanon, obliterating any globalist rhetoric, while Biden had no choice but to support it.

6) And most importantly: Trump did not surrender. He consolidated an unprecedented level of support within the Republican Party, radicalized the populist agenda, and, in effect, gave rise to a distinct ideology.

The main thesis of this emerging ideology was that *globalism has failed* — its crisis is not a fabrication by enemies or propaganda but reality itself.

Therefore, the U.S. should follow the path of Samuel Huntington rather than Francis Fukuyama, return to realism in international relations, restore America's foundational identity, abandon woke ideology and perversions, and reset its ideological framework to the classical liberalism of its early days, infused with protectionism and an unapologetic dose of nationalism.

This became the project of MAGA — "Make America Great Again."

The Deep State Shifts Priorities

Since Trump managed to solidify his ideological position within the American intellectual and political landscape, the Deep State refused to let the Democrats eliminate him.

Biden, weakened by his cognitive decline, failed the "Build Back Better" test and convinced no one. As a result, the Deep State acknowledged the reality of globalism's crisis and the collapse of its previous methods.

Thus, it allowed Trump to be elected, even permitting him to surround himself with a radical faction of ideological Trumpists, including figures such as:

- Elon Musk

- JD Vance

- Peter Thiel

- Robert Kennedy Jr.

- Tulsi Gabbard

- Kash Patel

- Pete Hegseth

- Tucker Carlson

- Even Alex Jones.

The key point: By recognizing Trump, the Deep State accepted the necessity of a fundamental revision of U.S. global strategy — in ideology, geopolitics, diplomacy, and governance.

From now on, everything is subject to revision.

Trumpism and populism are not glitches, not accidental disruptions, but reflections of the deep and *irreversible crisis of globalism.*

This new Trump presidency is not just another partisan alternation between Democrats and Republicans within the Deep State's established globalist order.

It marks the beginning of a historic shift in American hegemony — one that redefines its ideology, strategy, and governing structures.

Post-Liberalism

Now, let us examine the emerging contours of Trumpism as an ideology.

Vice President JD Vance openly calls himself a "post-liberal."

This signifies a *total rupture* with the left-liberal order that has dominated the U.S. for decades.

The Deep State, which traditionally lacks a fixed ideology, now appears willing to experiment with revising liberalism — if not dismantling it entirely.

Before our eyes, Trumpism is taking shape as a distinct ideological force, fundamentally opposed to the dominant left-liberal order.

The Three Core Pillars of Trumpism

1) Rejection of globalism

2) Rejection of left-liberalism (progressivism)

3) Rejection of woke culture

Anti-Woke Agenda

Trumpists vehemently oppose woke ideology, which they see as an existential threat to American identity. Their opposition includes:

- Rejecting gender ideology and the legalization of perversions

- Rejecting critical race theory, which promotes resentment against whites

- Rejecting mass migration, including illegal immigration

- Rejecting cancel culture and liberal censorship

- Rejecting postmodernism.

Instead of these progressivist, anti-traditional liberal values, Trumpism advocates a return to *traditional American values* and a *civilizational identity rooted in the heritage of Western civilization.*

In place of gender fluidity, Trumpism asserts *biological reality*: only two sexes exist.

Transgenderism and the LGBT agenda are not social norms but marginal perversions.

Feminism and its attack on masculinity and patriarchy are rejected — and masculinity is restored to its rightful central place in society.

No one should apologize for being a man.

This is why Trumpism is often called the "Bro Revolution" — a revolution of men.

Here is the full, faithful translation of your text:

Rehabilitation of White Civilization

In stark contrast to what critical racial theory espouses, Trumpism champions the rehabilitation of White civilization. While there are some White racist proponents of Trumpism, they do not reflect the entire movement but rather are on the extreme fringes. Most White Trumpists are tolerant of other races as long as they do not demand repentance or apologies from Whites

Against Immigration

Trumpism demands strict limitations on immigration and a complete ban on illegal migrants, with their deportation. Trumpists call for a *unified national identity*: they believe that anyone arriving in Western societies from other civilizations and cultures must adopt the traditional values of their host country, rather than being left to their own devices, as liberal multiculturalism insists.

Trumpism is particularly harsh toward illegal immigrants and the mass influx of Latin American migrants, which is visibly altering the ethnic balance in entire U.S. states, where Latinos are becoming the majority. Additionally, Islamic communities — which continue to grow and categorically reject Western norms and values (especially given that liberals never required them to assimilate and instead indulged minority groups) — are a major concern.

From an economic standpoint, Trumpists hold extremely negative views on China and Chinese activities in the U.S. Many call for the outright confiscation of land and businesses owned by the Chinese in the country.

African Americans do not provoke strong rejection, but when they begin organizing into aggressive political movements, such as Black Lives Matter (BLM), and turn criminals and drug addicts into heroes (as in the case of George Floyd), Trumpists react firmly and decisively. It is evident that the Floyd case and his "canonization" will soon be reassessed.

Against Left-Liberal Censorship

Trumpists are united and determined in their opposition to left-liberal censorship. Under the guise of *political correctness* and *combatting extremism*, liberals constructed an elaborate system of manipulating public opinion, effectively abolishing freedom of speech — both in mainstream media and on social media platforms they control**.

Anyone who *even slightly deviated* from the left-liberal agenda was *immediately* labeled an "extremist right-winger," "racist," "fascist," or "Nazi" and subjected to exclusion, deplatforming, and even legal persecution — up to and including imprisonment.

Censorship gradually became totalitarian, with Trumpism — alongside other anti-globalist movements (particularly in Russia), as well as European populist movements and multipolarity advocates — becoming a primary target. Liberal elites openly regarded ordinary citizens as feebleminded and socially unconscious elements, redefining democracy not as "the rule of the majority" but as "the rule of minorities."

Anything that did not align with the left-liberal agenda was branded "fake news," "Putinist propaganda," "conspiracy theory," or "dangerous extremist views" requiring punitive measures.

Thus, the Overton window (the range of acceptable discourse) narrowed dramatically, and anything deviating from the woke, ultra-left liberal dogma was declared unacceptable, persecuted, and blocked. This applied to all key pillars of liberal-globalism: gender ideology, immigration, critical race theory, vaccination mandates, etc.

In practice, liberalism became totalitarian and entirely intolerant, and under the pretense of "inclusivity," it sought only to turn every individual into a liberal.

Trumpism *radically rejects all of this* and demands the restoration of true freedom of speech, which over the past few decades has been progressively dismantled. No ideology should be given special privileges, and the protection of free expression across the entire ideological spectrum — from the far right to the far left — has become a core principle of Trumpism.

Against Postmodernism

Trumpists also reject postmodernism, which is generally associated with progressive left-liberal movements in culture and the arts. However, Trumpism has not yet developed its own distinct cultural style; it currently limits itself to removing postmodernist culture from its pedestal and calling for a diversification of cultural expression.

In general, Trumpists counter postmodernism and its inherent nihilism with traditional values — religion, sports, family, morality, etc.

Most Trumpists are not sophisticated intellectuals and instead advocate relativizing the postmodernist dictatorship and revising the principle that degenerate art should be considered the norm.

However, some Trumpist thinkers propose *"hijacking" postmodernism from the left and constructing an alternative, right-wing postmodernism* — a so-called "postmodernism from the right." They advocate appropriating irony and deconstruction, turning these tactics against left-liberal dogmas and canons, which were previously used primarily against traditionalists and conservatives.

During Trump's first election campaign, his supporters organized themselves on the 4chan platform, launching a wave of ironic memes and absurdist narratives that mocked and deliberately provoked liberals.

Some thinkers (such as Curtis Yarvin and Nick Land) took this even further, advancing the concept of "The Dark Enlightenment" — a counter-liberal reinterpretation of modernity — and even *calling for the establishment of a monarchy in the U.S.*

Elon Musk and Postmodernism

In some ways, a postmodernist figure within Trump's circle is Elon Musk — a key figure in securing Trump's victory, who combines traditional values and right-wing politics with a futuristic vision and an emphasis on technological advancement.

Another major thinker in this vein is Peter Thiel, one of Silicon Valley's most influential entrepreneurs, who similarly embraces *the fusion of tradition and high-tech futurism.*

From Hayek to Soros and Back

From the perspective of left-liberals, the political history of humanity over the past century has moved from classical liberalism to its leftist and even extreme left-wing radical version. If classical liberals tolerated deviations only at the individual level, never elevating them to the status of norms, let alone laws, progressive liberals have done precisely that. Like the old liberals, they began to eradicate all forms of collective identity, pushing individualism to the point of absurdity.

This process can be traced through three key figures of 20th-century liberal ideology.

Friedrich von Hayek, the founder of neoliberalism, believed that all ideologies prescribing what a person should think or do should be rejected. This was still the old classical liberalism, celebrating absolute individual freedom and an unrestricted free market.

His student, Karl Popper, expanded on this critique of totalitarian ideologies such as fascism and communism, extending it to Plato and Hegel as well. In Popper's works, totalitarian undertones became evident: he labeled liberals and supporters of liberalism as the "open society" while calling all those who thought otherwise "enemies of the open society," prescribing their preemptive elimination — even *before* they could harm the "open society" or slow its emergence.

Popper's student George Soros took this one step further, advocating the overthrow of any illiberal regimes, supporting the most radical — often terrorist — movements opposing such regimes, and relentlessly punishing, criminalizing, and eliminating opponents of the "open society" even in the West itself. Soros declared personal enemies in figures such as Trump, Putin, Modi, Xi Jinping, Orbán, and others. Using vast fortunes amassed through financial speculation, he began an aggressive campaign against them. He became the mastermind behind color revolutions in Eastern Europe, the post-Soviet space, the Islamic world, and even parts of Southeast Asia and Africa. He fully supported brutal measures to restrict personal freedoms during the COVID-19 pandemic, promoting forced mass vaccination and harshly persecuting COVID dissenters. Thus, the new liberalism became openly totalitarian, extremist, and terroristic.

Trumpism seeks to reverse this sequence of Hayek-Popper-Soros and return to its origins — to the anti-totalitarian, permissive, and in some ways classical liberalism of Friedrich von Hayek. Some Trumpists go even further, calling for a return to the fundamental American traditionalism that predated the Civil War.

Our overview provides a general picture of Trumpist ideology. However, within this broader context, distinct, and at times antagonistic, factions are beginning to emerge. While all Trumpists generally share the aforementioned positions, they emphasize different aspects in various ways — sometimes even in directly conflicting manners.

One dividing line is what has recently been called the "conflict be-tween right-wing technocrats and right-wing traditionalists," or "the Tech Right vs. the Trad Right."

The undisputed leader and symbol of the right-wing technocrats is Elon Musk. He combines technological futurism (Tech Right), vision-ary promises of human colonization of Mars, and the advancement of new technologies with the promotion of conservative values and active, assertive support for right-wing populism. His stance is well known and is now closely watched throughout the West.

Even before Trump's inauguration, Musk began actively promoting a new right-wing conservative agenda on his platform, X, effectively positioning himself as a replacement for Soros. The latter had long woven a global network of left-liberal influence, bribing politicians and orchestrating regime changes not only in hostile nations but also in neutral and even friendly countries. Now, Musk has taken on this role, and he will likely be supported by Mark Zuckerberg, the creator of Meta, who recently joined the Trumpist camp and promised to eliminate woke censorship on his platforms Instagram and Facebook.

Musk, alongside PayPal co-founder Peter Thiel and Zuckerberg, represents the "right-wing technocrat" faction.

The Tech Right vs. the Trad Right

Within the U.S., however, a faction of Trumpists has already formed in opposition to them, led primarily by Steve Bannon, Trump's former national security advisor during his first term. Bannon and his follow-ers have been labeled "right-wing traditionalists" (Trad Right).

A major point of contention arose over granting residency to legal immigrants — an initiative supported by Musk but strongly opposed by Bannon. Bannon formulated a platform of American national-ism, a key electoral pillar for Trump, demanding stricter citizenship procedures and coining the slogan: "America for Americans!" Many supported Bannon, pointing out that Musk had only recently joined the conservative movement, whereas American nationalists had been fighting for these values for decades.

Thus, a schism has emerged within Trumpism between right-wing globalism, futurism, and technocracy on one side, and right-wing nationalism on the other. This debate was recently highlighted in a sharp and witty commentary by anti-woke American comedian Sam Hyde.

Pro-Israel vs. Anti-Israel Trumpists

Another major fault line has emerged between pro-Israel and anti-Israel Trumpists.

It is well known that Trump himself, along with Vice President JD Vance and Pete Hegseth — who has been nominated as Secretary of Defense in Trump's new administration — are staunch supporters of Israel. It is likely that Trump's election was partially a result of his pro-Israel stance and unwavering support for Benjamin Netanyahu. The Jewish lobby is extraordinarily powerful in the U.S.

At the same time, several realists — such as John Mearsheimer, Jeffrey Sachs, and the renowned nonconformist journalist and investigator Alex Jones — strongly reject this aspect of Trumpism. They argue that the U.S. should take a more sober approach to the balance of power in the Middle East and pursue its own strategic interests, which often do not align with those of Israel.

Moreover, individuals within Trump's camp may take different stances on these two axes. For example, Alex Jones, who is highly critical of Israel, supports Musk, while Steve Bannon, who opposes Musk, is aligned with the pro-Israel faction.

The Generational Theory

Finally, it is worth mentioning the generational theory, developed some time ago by authors William Strauss and Neil Howe. This theory provides valuable insight into where Trumpism fits within American political and social history.

According to this theory, the U.S. experiences a system of constantly recurring cycles — both large (approximately 85 years, the rough
length of a human lifespan) and small. Each large cycle (*saeculum*,
century) consists of four stages or "turnings," which can be seen as the
four seasons.

1) The first turning is called the "High," corresponding to spring.

2) The second turning is the "Awakening," corresponding to summer.

3) The third is the "Unraveling," corresponding to autumn.

4) The fourth is the "Crisis," corresponding to winter.

Each turning lasts approximately 21 years, and each is associated with
a specific generational archetype. This is why the theory is called the
"generational theory." It is often referenced when discussing terms
like "The Greatest Generation" (1900–1923), "The Silent Generation"
(1923–1943), "The Baby Boomer Generation" (1943–1963), "Generation
X" (1963–1984), "Generation Y" (1984–2004), or "Generation Z /
Millennials" (2004–2024).

In the Strauss-Howe theory, the 1940s to 1950s are described as the
first phase of a new large cycle. This is the first turning of the *saeculum*,
which the authors call the "High." This period is characterized by a
powerful mobilization of society, social cohesion, strengthening of institutions, and an era of enthusiasm, optimism, solidarity, and shared
values.

The second turning, the 1960s to 1970s, is the "Awakening." This
is a time of internal reflection — the era of hippies, psychedelics, and
spiritual quests. It is marked by a shift towards individualism and the
gradual erosion of social solidarity. This was the age of rock music and
the sexual revolution.

The third turning, the 1980s to 1990s, is the "Unraveling." It represents a transition from spiritual individualism to materialistic and
hedonistic individualism. Social bonds weaken, institutions decline,

and cultural pessimism rises. The hippie era and classic rock give way to punk ("No Future"), techno, and industrial music.

From the 2000s to the 2020s, we have been experiencing the final turning — the "Crisis." A defining moment of this phase was the terrorist attack on the World Trade Center in New York on 9/11. What followed were prolonged U.S. interventions in various global conflicts, the COVID-19 pandemic, and the war in Ukraine. The social fabric has completely unraveled. Optimism has vanished. Society is rapidly degenerating. This is the violent agony of a dying cycle. Incompetent leaders — both Republican and Democrat — have ruled the U.S., each more disastrous than the last: George W. Bush, the narcissistic half-black Barack Obama, and the senile, dementia-stricken Joe Biden.

Individualism has devolved into the legalization of perversions. This is the era of *woke* ideology, with its gender politics, post-humanism, and radical environmentalism.

Thus, from the perspective of generational theory, the 2024 election represents nothing less than the end of an era (*saeculum*). Trumpism embodies the transition into a new era and the beginning of its first turning — the new "High." All the tendencies of the previous cycle, particularly the "Crisis," are being dismantled. Liberalism in the form of woke ideology is being completely discarded.

A new cycle begins, bringing with it new principles, rules, and priorities. Trump marks the end of the "Crisis" and the transition to the "High."

When the generational theory was first introduced, it was met with relatively positive responses from critics. However, once liberals realized how seriously it undermined their authority and ideology, they launched a furious attack against it, trying to discredit it as unscientific.

Strangely enough, the debate over its validity ultimately played a role in the 2024 election and the Deep State's decision to allow Trump's victory. It is likely that some factions within the Deep State became familiar with Strauss-Howe's theory and found it to be quite realistic. If so, then the rapid dismantling of left-liberalism and its structures should not be seen as a temporary anomaly, after which a return to the previous trajectory will occur. On the contrary, such a return may never happen — at least if the theory is correct. And so far, it appears quite convincing.

The Geopolitics of Trumpism

Now let us turn to another aspect of Trumpism: its foreign policy. The key shift here is the transition from a globalist perspective to an America-centric and expansionist approach.

One of the clearest examples of this shift are Trump's statements about annexing Canada as the 51st state, purchasing Greenland, reclaiming control over the Panama Canal, and renaming the Gulf of Mexico to the "Gulf of America." These are all hallmarks of aggressive realism in international relations and, moreover, a return to the Monroe Doctrine after a century of dominance by Woodrow Wilson's doctrine.

The Monroe Doctrine of the 19th century prioritized U.S. control over North America, and to some extent South America, aiming to weaken and eliminate European influence in the Western Hemisphere. In contrast, Wilson's Doctrine, articulated after World War One, became the roadmap for American globalists, shifting the focus from the U.S. as a national state to its mission of spreading liberal democracy worldwide and maintaining its structures on a global scale. Under this framework, America itself was secondary to its international mission.

During the Great Depression, the U.S. temporarily abandoned Wilsonianism, but after World War Two, it returned in full force. In recent decades, this doctrine has dominated.

Under Wilsonianism, the ownership of Canada, Greenland, or the Panama Canal was irrelevant, as all were governed by liberal-democratic regimes controlled by the globalist elite.

Today, however, Trump is radically shifting this focus. The U.S. as a nation-state once again "matters," and it now demands obedience — not to the World Government (which Trump is effectively dismantling) — but to Washington, the U.S., and Trump himself, as the charismatic leader of the new "High" era.

A map of the U.S. with 51 states (including Puerto Rico), Greenland, and the Panama Canal vividly illustrates this pivot from Wilsonianism back to the Monroe Doctrine.

The Dismantling of Globalist Regimes in Europe

Perhaps the most surprising development — one that has left the West stunned — is the speed with which Trumpists, even before fully consolidating power, have begun implementing their agenda on the international stage.

Elon Musk, through his platform X, launched an active campaign in December 2024 to remove leaders who were unfavorable to the newly Trumpist United States. Previously, such regime-change operations had been the domain of Soros-backed globalist structures. Now, Musk has wasted no time in doing the same — but in favor of anti-globalists and European populists such as Germany's Alternative for Germany (AfD) led by Alice Weidel, Nigel Farage in Britain, and Marine Le Pen in France.

Denmark's government faced similar pressure after refusing to cede Greenland voluntarily. In Canada, Prime Minister Justin Trudeau resisted the idea of his country becoming the 51st U.S. state.

European globalists — remnants of the old network — are in complete confusion, objecting to this direct U.S. interference in European politics. But Musk and the Trumpists have responded bluntly:

"No one objected when Soros did the same thing in favor of globalists. So now, accept our version!"

If the U.S. is the master of the world, then obey — just as you did under Obama, Biden, and Soros, that is, under the Deep State.

Musk, along with Thiel, Zuckerberg, and other tech moguls, has begun dismantling the globalist system — primarily in Europe — by supporting and empowering populist leaders aligned with Trumpist ideas.

The easiest transition has been for Hungary under Viktor Orbán, Slovakia under Robert Fico, and Italy under Giorgia Meloni, as these governments already aligned with traditional values and had varying degrees of opposition to globalism.

However, in other countries, Trumpists are prepared to change regimes by any means necessary — just as their globalist predecessors did.

Trumpists are toppling liberals and globalists in Europe. Ultimately, they seek to consolidate the West as a unified geopolitical and ideological civilization. In essence, they are building a full-fledged American Empire.

Anti-China Stance

Another fundamental aspect of Trumpist international policy is opposition to China. To Trumpists, China represents everything they despise in left-wing liberalism and globalism: leftist ideology and internationalism. They see China as embodying both of these elements and traditionally associate it with the policies of their own American globalists. Of course, modern China is a far more complex phenomenon, but the anti-China consensus among Trumpists is based on the belief that China, as a stronghold of a non-White and non-Western civilization, has exploited globalization to its advantage — not only elevating itself to the status of an independent pole of power but also acquiring a significant portion of American industry, business, and land. The outsourcing of manufacturing to Southeast Asia in search of cheaper labor has deprived the U.S. of its industrial potential and economic sovereignty, making the country dependent on external sources. Moreover, China's distinct ideology renders it inherently unmanageable by the U.S.

Trumpists place all the blame for China's economic miracle on their own globalists, making China their primary enemy.

Compared to China, Russia becomes a secondary issue and simply fades from focus. China is now enemy number one, and once again, all blame for global disorder is assigned to American globalists.

Pro-Israel Trend

The second most important theme of Trumpist foreign policy is support for Israel and the "far-right" factions within Israel. While we have seen that this is not a universal consensus among Trumpists — since there is also an anti-Israel segment — overall, the main vector remains pro-Israel. This position is rooted in the Protestant theory of Judeo-Christianity, which anticipates the arrival of the Jewish Messiah as a moment when Jews will convert to Christianity, as well as in a general rejection of Islam. Trumpist Islamophobia fuels their solidarity with Israel (and vice versa), making this one of the most significant aspects of their policy in the Middle East.

In this regard, Trumpists view the Shia pole of Islam, which is the most actively anti-Israel, as the greatest evil. Hence their strong hostility toward Iran, Iraqi Shiites, the Houthis in Yemen, and the Alawites in Syria. Trumpism maintains a staunchly anti-Shia stance and is generally aligned with right-wing Zionism.

Against Latinos

The Latino factor is a crucial issue in U.S. domestic politics. Here again, Samuel Huntington is of great importance, as he warned several decades ago that the greatest threat to North American identity and its core WASP (White Anglo-Saxon Protestant) type comes from the massive influx of Latin American immigrants, who have an entirely different Catholic-Latin identity. According to Huntington, for a time, Anglo-Saxons were able to assimilate other ethnic groups within the American "melting pot," but with the mass influx of Latinos, this has become impossible.

As a result, anti-immigration sentiment in the U.S. has taken on a more specific focus — animosity towards mass migration from Latin

American countries. Trump initiated the construction of the Great Wall along the southern border during his first presidential term to curb this wave.

This also shapes the Trumpist attitude towards Latin American nations: they are generally perceived as "leftist" and as sources of criminal migration. A return to the Monroe Doctrine means that the U.S. must exert tighter control over Latin American countries. This directly leads to an escalation of tensions with Mexico and, in particular, explains the demand for full control over the Panama Canal.

Russia Is Irrelevant, Ukraine Even More So

In Trumpist international policy, Russia is seen as a minor factor. Unlike globalists, Trumpists do not harbor ideological or automatic Russophobia, but neither do they feel much sympathy for Russia. Among Trumpists, there is a small group of Russophiles who believe that Russia is part of White Christian civilization and that it would be foolish and reckless to push it further into China's embrace. However, they remain a minority. For most Trumpists, Russia simply does not matter. It does not pose serious economic competition (unlike China), it has no significant diaspora in the U.S., and the conflict with Ukraine is viewed as a regional issue of little consequence, for which globalists (the enemies of Trumpists) are to blame.

Of course, it would be beneficial to end the conflict in Ukraine, but if this cannot be achieved quickly, Trumpists will leave the matter to European globalist regimes, which will exhaust themselves and weaken in the process — an outcome that only serves the Trumpist agenda.

As for Ukraine, it is not seen as an important or significant player at all. The only relevance it holds is in the broader investigation into the corrupt dealings of the Obama and Biden administrations.

Passive Multipolarity

It is worth examining the attitude of Trumpism towards multipolarity. It is unlikely that the theory of a multipolar world is entirely acceptable to them. Trumpism is a new edition of American hegemony, but here unipolarity takes on a completely different content and nature compared to the globalists' version. At the center of the world system stand the United States and its traditional values — that is, the *White Christian West*, which is quite patriarchal but simultaneously recognizes freedom, individual rights, and the market. Everyone else is offered either to follow the West or to remain outside its zone of prosperity and development. This is no longer an inclusive order but a limited exclusivity. The West is a club that one must strive hard to enter.

Therefore, Trumpists are completely indifferent to other civilizations. If they insist on their own way — so be it. That is their loss. But if they wish to join the West, they must pass a series of rigorous tests. And even then, they will remain second-tier societies.

In other words, this is not an active and affirmative multipolarity but a passive and permissive one: "If you cannot be the West, then just be yourselves." Trumpists do not seek to build a multipolar world, but they have nothing against it. It will emerge on its own as a residual phenomenon. Not everyone is destined to be the West; the rest can either strive for this goal or accept that they will remain as they are.

Internal American Multipolarity

A key element of Trumpist ideology is its primary focus on domestic issues in the U.S. The slogans "MAGA" and "America First!" highlight this emphasis. Thus, Trumpists encounter the phenomenon of multipolarity more in domestic politics than in foreign policy. Yes, they seek to establish U.S. hegemony on new ideological foundations, but domestic policy remains their priority. And within America itself, Trumpism confronts multipolarity in the form of distinct civilizations.

Multipolar world theory identifies seven main civilizations:

1) Western

2) Russian-Eurasian

3) Chinese

4) Indian

5) Islamic

6) African

7) Latin American.

They form a *heptarchy*, where some poles are already consolidated as *civilization states*, while others remain in a virtual state. This is what Huntington (with the addition of the Japanese-Buddhist civilization) described.

In foreign policy, Trumpism is not particularly concerned with the heptarchy. Unlike the globalists, Trumpists no longer see it as their goal to sabotage the process of multipolarity or attack BRICS, but they are also clearly not interested in promoting it. Thus, the heptarchy becomes most relevant in domestic politics. And here, in contrast, its presence is strongly felt. The issue arises with the large and sometimes very significant diasporas in the United States. Since woke norms and inclusivity have been abolished, it is once again possible in the U.S. to openly discuss race, ethnicity, and religious identities.

Thus, as we have already seen, the Latin American diaspora becomes a major problem. It threatens the core WASP identity of the U.S., actively eroding it. This logically leads to the demonization of everything associated with Latin America — ethnic mafias, waves of illegal immigrants crossing the border, Latin American drug cartels, human trafficking, and so on. Latin America is present *inside* the U.S., and its image is largely negative and destructive. As a result, the Latin American pole will inevitably be viewed in a negative light, which is already manifesting in escalating tensions with Mexico. The Monroe Doctrine, which Trump is reviving, presupposes the absolute dominance of the U.S. in the Western Hemisphere, which directly contradicts the formation of an independent Latin American pole. Trumpists will be more or less radical in their approach to this issue.

The second major internal factor is the rising wave of *Sinophobia*. China is the main economic and financial competitor of the U.S., and the significant Chinese presence within the American economy only intensifies this issue. This pole of the heptarchy — both inside and outside the U.S. — will also be viewed through the lens of hostility.

The Islamic world has traditionally been an adversary for American right-wing conservatives. Trumpist Islamophobia is also a key reason for their unconditional support of Israel, regardless of how extreme its actions may be. Muslim communities are widely represented in the U.S. and the West in general, and in the eyes of Trumpists, they are an enemy.

India is viewed entirely differently. Today, there is a huge Indian diaspora in the U.S., and in some sectors, particularly in Silicon Valley, Indians dominate. Some of Trump's closest allies, such as Vivek Ramaswamy and Kash Patel, are Indian. Vice President JD Vance's wife is Indian. Tulsi Gabbard, ethnically a Maori from Hawaii, has convert-ed to Hinduism. While the nationalist segment of Trumpists — such as Steve Bannon and Ann Coulter — have recently begun voicing concerns about the growing influence of Indians in the U.S. and in Trump's circle, overall, Trumpists have a favorable view of India as a pole both within and outside the U.S. Furthermore, they do not hide their desire to make India the primary hub of cheap industrial labor, replacing China. Thus, their attitude towards Indian civilization is generally positive.

Africa as such does not concern Trumpists much, but once again, this pole is understood through the lens of the African-American population in the U.S. The racial consolidation of African Americans in opposition to Whites — something that the globalists actively en-couraged — is seen as a threat. Thus, Trumpists generally seek further assimilation of African Americans and oppose their separatism. This will also affect the regulation of immigration from Africa to the U.S.

Another member of the heptarchy is Russia. But unlike the other civilizations, Russians in the U.S. are extremely limited in number.

They do not form a significant ethnic mass and most often fully integrate into American sociocultural structures, blending in with the White population alongside other European groups.

Thus, Trumpists struggle to conceptualize Russia as a distinct pole and usually do so in retrospect. The Soviet Union was once the main geopolitical adversary of the U.S. and the West. Sometimes this image is projected onto modern Russia, but this hostile perception was so aggressively exploited by globalists in the previous stage that it has now been completely drained of meaning. For the new Trumpist course, Russia is more of an afterthought than an adversary. Although within Trumpism, there are opposing poles — both Russophobic and Russophile (though the latter is less represented).

Trumpists' stance on multipolarity, therefore, will largely be shaped by *internal* American dynamics.

Thus, Trumpism is an ideology. It has both political-philosophical and geopolitical dimensions. Over time, it will become more sharply defined and distinct, but even now, its main features are not difficult to outline.

THE GREAT OCTOBER
REVOLUTION OF
DONALD TRUMP

"Someone Like Putin"

WE HAD BEEN WAITING for Trump's victory, counting on it, though we did not always openly admit it. On the contrary, we often concealed our expectations in various ways, including trying not to harm Trump himself. I believe this is why our President made his statement in support of Harris — just to "knock on wood" and avoid jinxing things. And also, not to expose the candidate who meant a completely different, new perspective for our relations with the West, with the U.S., and for the global balance of power in general.

Trump is not just the Republican candidate — he is by no means an ordinary candidate for America, for the Republican Party, or for world politics. Trump is a world revolution. A Conservative Revolution. And the fact that he has now managed to come back — after having already won once, withstanding all the blows during Biden's presidency, and now triumphantly reclaiming victory — means that his rise is not an accident. No one can claim anymore that it was just a "glitch in the system." No, this is a trend, a fundamental trajectory.

Trump cemented this trend by choosing JD Vance as his vice president — the first time in American politics that someone at such a high level has explicitly stated that their ideology is "*post-liberal* right." There is nothing more significant than this statement from Vance.

"Post-liberal right" means true right-wing politics — those who stand for traditional values rather than big capital. The right in the fundamental sense, conservative right, "illiberal" right, or as Vance himself calls it, "post-liberal." The fact that Trump won alongside Vance, a young ideologue of the *Conservative Revolution*, means that this trend is here to stay.

What has happened is not just an accident. It is not just a matter of Trump having survived — having not been imprisoned, assassinated, or destroyed despite eight years of relentless demonization from democratic fanatics who ceaselessly labeled him a "fascist" and a "Putinist." And that is why today, we can confidently say that "Putinism" has won in the U.S. — America has voted for... "*we want someone like Putin.*"

Do Not Expect Miracles but Kiev Must Be Taken

Russia should not expect miracles from Trump and his new administration. We must win the war in Ukraine, liberate the entire territory of this former country from the Nazi regime. Regardless of Trump's victory or anything else, this imperative remains unchanged. Just as the ancient Roman consul Cato the Elder used to say, "Carthage must be destroyed," in our case, "Kiev must be taken." And our troops must march all the way to Lvov, liberating the entire territory of former Ukraine from the Nazi yoke.

Of course, the terms that Trump offers us will also be very important. But that is still a secondary issue, concerning how we will formalize our continued march towards victory. Here, we must act shrewdly, cleverly, and wisely — but always with the understanding that victory is paramount.

We should also take note of how Trump is perceived in Kiev. Trump's son, Donald Jr., as well as JD Vance, Elon Musk, and especially Tucker Carlson — some of the most prominent figures supporting Trump — openly despise the Ukrainian Nazi regime. They rightly believe that Zelensky and his junta were entirely created by the

Democratic administration and that behind them stand the globalists who dragged the West and the U.S. into a failed adventure in Ukraine.

Kiev, in turn, pays them back in kind. Many of these figures are already listed in Ukraine's "*Myrotvorets*" database, which is banned in Russia — a website where Ukrainian Nazis gleefully publish information about their enemies, effectively calling for their physical elimination through terrorist methods. Donald Trump Jr. and Tucker Carlson are already listed there. In other words, a significant part of Trump's future administration is, according to the Ukrainian Nazi regime, marked for liquidation.

I believe this will all soon come to an end. No, this does not mean a direct withdrawal of U.S. support for Kiev. It is unlikely that Trump will immediately cut everything off and tell the Russians, "Do whatever you want with this rabble." But the Republicans now in power will, for a time, simply forget about the Ukrainian war. Maybe even forever. They will say, "We have other, far more important domestic problems: the decay of American society, the corruption of the ruling class, the rampant corruption, and the assault on values that are fundamental to Americans."

At the same time, Trump will likely continue supporting Netanyahu and his aggressive actions in the Middle East — something that is, of course, bad news for the Arab population of the region. He will also intensify America's trade war with China. Perhaps he will offer more active support to South Korea in its confrontation with North Korea. In other words, Trump's victory does not mean that all problems will be resolved. But what is clear is that he will shift attention away from the Ukrainian conflict. This is obvious based on the simplest pragmatic considerations — because neither America nor Trump himself stands to gain anything from it.

It is evident that Trump will place the blame for everything that has happened squarely on Biden. It is even possible that Biden, Kamala Harris, and their entire clique — who unleashed the bloody carnage in Ukraine — will be put on trial. Or perhaps they will be spared. But that is another matter. What is certain is that under Trump and Vance, Ukraine will drop to the 15th place among the White House's policy priorities. And this presents us with an opportunity — one that we must seize.

Hypothetically, Trump might present Moscow with a harsh ultimatum, demanding that we immediately halt the Special Military Operation. However, this is highly unlikely because, as a realist and pragmatist, he fully understands that Putin will not comply. And what would happen then? Trump promised to stop the war, but he would fail to do so. Therefore, it would be better to set aside such promises — at least until our victory is secured.

Trump will not engage in the exorcism of demons from the deranged Kiev regime. Confronting this real Nazism is our burden, our fate, our trial, and our tragedy. We must resolve it ourselves. As for global affairs, Trump's return to power is the only way to avert a world war, prevent nuclear apocalypse, and transition towards the construction of a multipolar world — without a direct collision with Western hegemony. Trump has his own vision of how America should become great again — not through globalism, not through Democratic imperialism, not through imposing a single model on all nations, as liberals and Democrats have attempted to do, first and foremost upon American society itself.

The Schism in the Deep State

Trump would not have been able to win — or more precisely, no one would have acknowledged his victory — if it were not for the divisions within the U.S. deep state. On the eve of the elections, I published an article in the popular American conservative magazine *Man's World* about this very split, highlighting how the globalist "Plan A," followed by all previous Democratic and Republican candidates alike, had reached a dead end.

As a result, Trump now has a unique opportunity to implement a "Plan B," one centered on a just multipolar world order. This is why the recent triumphant BRICS summit in Kazan was not just a magnificent gesture but also an effective intervention in the American elections. Trump has received a blank check from the deep state to attempt a different strategy for preserving America's leadership — one that does not involve direct confrontation with the multipolar world.

Summing Up: Trump's Ideology

It is crucial to emphasize Trump's ideology. He is not a liberal, not a globalist; he runs counter to the trend that the global West follows today: LGBT, post-humanism, moral decay, total degeneration. This post-humanist, post-gender reality is backed by the most powerful ideological, economic, financial, and cultural centers: Bernard-Henri Lévy, Yuval Harari, Klaus Schwab — not just American Democrats but the globalist liberal elite of all nations. It is no coincidence that Yuval Harari has said that Trump's victory would mean "the end of everything." It would be a global catastrophe for what liberals consider the only path forward. And this catastrophe has already begun — a catastrophe for the bearers of the Satanic agenda.

What Does This Mean for Us?

Under these circumstances, it is vital that we do not forget ourselves. We must strengthen our sovereignty, completely purge the "sixth column" of those who support globalist liberal development, and redouble our efforts to defend our values and construct a multipolar world based on the sovereignty of civilization states.

Russia must firmly establish itself as a pole of power. If it does, then the realist Trump will sooner or later be forced to acknowledge this reality. That will be our victory and the guarantee of our future — a challenging, yet truly Russian sovereign future.

TRUMP 2.0: THE BEGINNING

Trump's Great America: The Pre-Inauguration Concert

Transcript of the program Escalation with Alexander Dugin *on Radio Sputnik, January 20, 2025.*

Tatyana Ladyaeva (Sputnik): Less than eight hours remain until Donald Trump officially assumes office. However, before delving into the consequences of this event, it is appropriate to discuss the pre-inauguration concert. This event included two separate concerts: one in support of Trump and another organized by his detractors, who gathered with their slogans, rallies, and calls to action. A notable controversy arose regarding the participation of key celebrities in the anti-Trump concert, raising questions about the nature of their involvement.

Alexander Dugin: It is important to note that such comparisons are inappropriate. As the well-known and influential commentator Jack Posobiec stated, a regime change has taken place in America.

Of course, one could argue that Kamala Harris, the ailing Biden, and several celebrities from P. Diddy's circle — participants in Satanic orgies — perhaps indeed gathered to support one another, much like Russian foreign agents and expatriates who seek to divert attention from the prevailing political landscape. However, their time has passed, and they are now forced to find new places in other countries.

This event can be compared to a clandestine gathering of the banned-in-Russia musician Makarevich with Galkin and Pugacheva. Yes, this group of foreign agents attempted to draw attention to themselves and, in doing so, distract from the true coronation ball, which became a symbol of victory for America's new course. Nevertheless, their attempts appear to be nothing more than minor protests against the truly powerful event that is Trump's inauguration. Perhaps some representatives of the LGBT community donned provocative costumes for this small demonstration, but they were quickly removed from the scene. This scenario resembles the actions of Alexei Navalny and other relocated dissidents.

In contrast, Trump's coronation ball was a landmark event, highlighted by his signature dance to the song "YMCA" by the Village People. "YMCA" is the anthem of conservative Christian youth. This performance was a challenge to left-liberal ideology and transgender activists who had previously dominated American politics.

The regime change that Posobiec spoke of was clearly reflected in the speeches and appearance of the ball's guests. Notably, Vice President JD Vance and his wife Usha, a Hindu, along with other attendees, dressed in a traditional, high-style manner, reflecting a departure from the liberal-democratic aesthetic. Democracy and liberalism no longer exist as a style in America. The most "democratic" among them all was Elon Musk with his son. This young Trump supporter (Musk's son) was the only person not dressed in strict, traditional attire.

We have understood American culture as a culture of degeneration and perversion, reflected in terms such as "woke" and "DEI" (Diversity, Equity, and Inclusion). However, none of that was present at the coronation ball; instead, a true ballroom atmosphere prevailed. It was a different kind of America — one that was not stingy with its promises. But those promises were quite ominous. They heralded the beginning of a new era in which America dramatically shifts its ideological content.

All the ball's participants spoke about this: Megyn Kelly, Elon Musk, and Robert Kennedy, grandson of the late President John F. Kennedy. Promises were made to change almost everything from day one, including the abolition of LGBT rights and the recognition of only two God-given sexes: male and female. Among other promises was the expulsion of all illegal migrants, affecting millions of people whom the previous liberal-democratic administration had artificially brought into the U.S. to expand its electoral base. Trump promised the imminent publication of the Epstein and P. Diddy lists, which would undoubtedly implicate the leadership of the Democratic Party and those protesting against Trump, including both those who have already gone into exile and those who may do so in the future.

Kennedy, who will oversee healthcare, promised to withdraw from the World Health Organization (WHO) and hold Dr. Fauci accountable, accusing him of criminal vaccination and fabricating a false pandemic in the interests of Big Pharma. Kash Patel, potential head of the FBI, also pledged to bring Biden to justice, as Trump's supporters believe he rigged the previous election. In reality, in 2020, the American majority gave its preference to Trump.

Current events in America highlight a shift in the political landscape. It is worth noting that Elon Musk has declared war on Macron, Starmer, and Scholz. The inauguration was also attended by representatives of right-wing populist parties from Britain and France, such as Marion Le Pen and Nigel Farage, as well as members of Alternative for Germany (AfD). This indicates the emergence of a new America, one in which traditional values have triumphed.

It is interesting to note that traditional values at this coronation ball were infused with an unprecedented surge of fresh energy. It seems that a significant portion of American society had long been in a state of cultural, political, and media compression — like a coiled spring. Left-liberal globalist elites exerted pressure on them, imposing the study of critical race theory in schools, where White people were already being declared an inferior race and forced to repent. The woke agenda and cancel culture compressed the American spring to its limit.

If one were to believe the mainstream press and key speakers of the previous administration, American society essentially did not exist — it was treated as a marginal phenomenon, labeled as "far-right." However, Musk asserts that these are not "far-right" extremists but rather the entire American people who were relegated to the margins and branded as extremists. And with the current changes, it is becoming clear that this society, like a compressed spring, is now rapidly expanding.

Of course, no one can predict the future with certainty. However, the transformations that have taken place since Trump's election victory last year are already significant. While they may not always turn out to be favorable, this is an entirely different situation.

Naive and Irresponsible to Underestimate the Potential of the Changes We Are Witnessing in the Western World

There are no longer just one, but two Wests: the West of American Trumpism and the West of globalism. The collective West has split into two poles. But what does this mean for us? Could this be an opportunity to move beyond the current confrontation?

We remain in a state of opposition to the West and to America, which, even under Trump's leadership, remains a key force behind the conflict in Ukraine.

This does not mean that everything will go smoothly. Tremendous changes have taken place, the significance of which cannot be ignored. At the same time, we must not conclude that our relations with America will now suddenly improve.

Traditional Values, Sovereignty, Statehood, and Civilization in the Context of the U.S. Elections

For at least the past five centuries — if not longer — the West has been a colonialist entity, a hegemonic force seeking to subjugate the rest of the planet. This is nothing new, and of course, Trump in no way negates the West's drive for dominance, its will to power on a global scale. What has changed before our eyes is simply the form of American and Western hegemony — radically and qualitatively.

For the past thirty years, Western hegemony has been advancing under the banner of left-liberal ideology. According to this paradigm, the entire world was supposed to become a unified entity under a global government. The concept of the state was to be abolished, national armies disbanded, and sovereignty eliminated. Only a single global market and isolated individuals would remain. Countries would cease to exist — hence the ideology of human rights, the push for mass illegal migration (because it no longer mattered whether migration was legal or illegal, only that everyone lived together in a planetary melting pot).

At the same time, not only were states dismantled, but so too were cultures, languages, and religions — all of which were ridiculed and eradicated. Gender was abolished, and history was rewritten to fit new rules, creating an entirely new humanity based on liberal and ultra-liberal ideology. This was the reality — until very recently.

Trump's first presidency disrupted this trajectory, calling this entire agenda into question. Biden promised to restore it; his campaign slogan, "Build Back Better," meant a return to the globalist left-liberal plan. However, he failed this test — he botched his mission by escalating the war in Ukraine and failing to improve conditions within America itself. This was not just Biden's personal failure but the failure of the entire system that had upheld Western hegemony for the past thirty years.

Now, this hegemony is taking on a different shape. Of course, it will still be hegemony. The West will maintain its central role in global affairs but without the dissolution of nation-states, without open borders, without the imposition of a World Government, and without forcing post-humanist, transhumanist, and transgender values on everyone.

This is an entirely different model. Hegemony will persist, and we must be prepared for that — but it will be a different kind of hegemony. We must soberly recognize which models and mechanisms will dominate this new Western hegemony (the new Trumpist world order): without a World Government, without globalization, without hyper-individualism, and without the imposition of the LGBT agenda as well as woke and DEI (Diversity, Equity, Inclusion), all of which have dominated for decades. Nevertheless, this will pose a serious challenge. If we show even the slightest weakness and cling to outdated norms of a world order that has already been swept away by the tide of change, we may face severe consequences.

Trump has, in effect, dismantled this globalist world order from within. We have entered a new era with a new America and a new West — this is a major challenge. The key takeaway is that we must be strong, sovereign, and completely independent from the West. We must defend the foundations of our state and civilization, assert our own value system, insist on our sovereignty, and strengthen our military-strategic potential.

We must abandon the illusion of liberal democracy, which was imposed on us by the Cold War victors over thirty years ago and nearly led us to catastrophe.

Now, this liberal democracy has been rejected both in the West and within our own country. There is no longer any justification for continuing this farce of liberalism and democracy in Russia.

That being said, the speed of the transformations now unfolding in the West presents a serious challenge for us. We are still moving rather slowly on the path of returning to tradition, to our Orthodox Christian roots, to the restriction of illegal immigration, and to the strengthening of our sovereignty — both in industry and in culture. However, our course remains steady and consistent.

At this moment, we cannot continue implementing the patriotic reforms initiated by Vladimir Putin 25 years ago — reforms that only entered their active phase after the start of the Special Military Operation — at the same pace as before.

This raises a very serious question. We have morally supported the conservative right-populist movements and parties in Europe that were largely pro-Russian and opposed to war with us. However, in a short time, Trump has managed to reorient them toward himself. We were hesitant and too reserved, afraid to offend the globalists and liberals, afraid to cross certain lines — whereas Trump fears nothing. In a sense, this is a slap in the face for us. We have long declared our commitment to traditional values, but Trump expresses this commitment *boldly, vividly, and unapologetically*.

In my view, this is one of the main challenges we face. We must not change course — on the contrary, we are moving in the right direction, and we embarked on this path *far earlier* than America. We have made great progress, but our sovereign reforms — post-liberal and even post-democratic — are being carried out timidly and almost shamefully, as if disguised. It is time for us to turn fully towards this course and declare: *You are an empire, but so are we.*

If you wish to control the territories in your sphere — Canada, the Panama Canal, Greenland — then we likewise seek to control our security zone — Ukraine, our *51st state*, if you will. Only then will we be understood.

The new leadership in America will understand us because it will act in much the same way. However, this does not mean that despite certain ideological similarities between Russia and Trump's America, we are fully aligned. Our similarities lie only in our shared orientation towards post-liberalism, traditional values, and the rejection of the globalist and left-liberal ideology. In this respect, we indeed find common ground, but there are also significant differences.

The most important distinction is that our actions must be *independent of America*. We must act as the great sovereign Russian Empire once did — the Eurasian Empire that asserted its interests, its spheres of influence, and its nuclear sovereignty. We must no longer adhere to the globalist norms imposed upon us.

Our course is absolutely correct, as laid out by our President. However, the speed of its implementation, the depth of reforms, and the restructuring of the elites raise certain concerns. Meanwhile, in America, a real change of course is occurring — a "regime change operation," as Posobiec put it.

At the coronation ball, we saw an entirely new set of political figures — none of whom included Boris Johnson or the classic representatives of the Republican Party. Practically no one from the old guard was present. Trump is carrying out a *personnel revolution*, and with him come passionate, fresh, bold, and dynamic individuals. These new figures may make mistakes, say too much, or act too extravagantly — but if they are rational, they can correct their errors and return to constructive action. What distinguishes them is their energy and drive.

At the same time, our reforms are often entrusted to the useless remnants of the old elite. These individuals do not operate by the principles of traditional values and do not act in the interest of creating the new Russian Empire that our President speaks of. Instead, they are guided by cynical motivations, reminiscent of the lyrics of a Instasamka song.[1]

As a result, despite the correctness of our course, we face challenges in its implementation and a lack of real depth in our transformation.

---

1   Editor's note: Instasamka (real name: Daria Zoteeva) is a Russian rapper and social media influencer known for her provocative and often vulgar lyrics. Her music is characterized by themes of money, materialism, self-indulgence, and explicit content.

"Slow and Steady Wins the Race?"

If we were alone in the world, then perhaps this saying would be true. In general, Russians are a gentle, calm, and contemplative people. Sometimes we can work brilliantly, but we also enjoy not working. We can achieve glorious victories, but we can also forget that we are surrounded by enemies.

Our people operate in several modes, and not all of them are suitable or beneficial in all circumstances. At times, we are slow and unhurried — sometimes this helps us, but in other situations, it can become a fatal mistake.

We have now entered an era of interaction with a rapidly evolving conservative-revolutionary America. The speed of changes occurring in the United States today is a challenge to us.

We cannot afford to just sit and watch. Under different circumstances, perhaps such an approach would have been justified. But if we do not secure our starting positions in this new great-power competition *right now*, we risk running out of time.

At this moment, unfortunately, the saying "slow and steady wins the race" does not apply to us. Moreover, this is an ironic saying. There is a paradox in it — a kind of Russian koan. Sometimes it holds true but far from always.

Taste, style, and an understanding of life and its nuances require us to adapt different proverbs, rules, and examples to different situations. In one case, a proverb may reflect the wisdom of our people, but in another, it may be completely inappropriate. In my opinion, we are already significantly behind.

Even our President has said that we should have started in 2014, but once again, we hesitated. The President acknowledges that "slow and steady" does not always win the race. Sometimes, slow and steady means losing everything.

The conditions of our conflict in Ukraine are, to a large extent, a result of our sluggishness, not our speed.

When in 2022, we made a sudden push, our most strategically vital positions were captured immediately. Yes, we were not fully prepared. In those first days of the Special Military Operation, we had to retreat. But even so, we now control almost four regions precisely because we did not hesitate in launching the SMO — even though it was already delayed.

Now, we must *dramatically accelerate* the process of replacing the ruling elites. These elites are unfit for purpose; they are "conservative" in the worst sense of the word — not proactive but merely reactionary. They only respond to events instead of anticipating them.

We need a forward-thinking, truly Russian, traditionalist, and conservative elite. We need *Russian dynamism* in our state-building. And in my view, this is the demand of our time.

USAID Destroyed

The liquidation of the United States Agency for International Development (USAID) is an event whose significance can hardly be overstated. When the Soviet Union abolished the Comintern (Third International) and later the Cominform, structures that advocated the ideological interests of the USSR on a global scale, it marked the beginning of the end for the international Soviet system. Although the Council for Mutual Economic Assistance (COMECON) and the Warsaw Pact Organization existed until 1991, their demise was essentially predetermined during Khrushchev's time.

Something similar is happening today in America, as USAID was the main operational structure for the implementation of globalist projects. Essentially, it was the primary transmission belt for globalism as an ideology aimed at the worldwide imposition of liberal democracy, market economics, and human rights, while dismantling sovereign states and overthrowing regimes capable of resisting this on a global scale.

Through this agency, globalism was embedded in various countries. That is why USAID was financed with a substantial portion of the U.S. federal budget: about 1% — amounting to $50 billion annually. When you factor in subsidies from other globalist structures, this figure at least doubles. Thus, approximately 2% of the American treasury was spent on this agency each year. One can only imagine the material resources this organization possessed. Additionally, it was closely integrated with a certain segment of the Central Intelligence Agency (most USAID branches worldwide served as cover for CIA activities, into which globalist ideas were actively embedded).

After sweeping out the previous U.S. political leadership — super-globalists — Donald Trump began purging the CIA of representatives from this globalist structure. The banning of USAID is a critical, fundamental move, the importance of which, as I said, cannot be overstated. This is especially true because countries like Ukraine largely depend on this agency, receiving significant funding through it. All Ukrainian media, NGOs, and ideological structures were financed by USAID. The same applies to almost the entire liberal opposition in the post-Soviet space, as well as liberal regimes in various countries, including Maia Sandu's Moldovan administration and many European political regimes, which were also on USAID's payroll.

And suddenly, all of this collapses. Sure, some committed liberals will continue their activities out of ideological conviction, but they are a very small percentage. The vast majority of liberalism and global liberal networks operate on the principle of "money for loyalty." But whose money funds this liberal "loyalty"? It is USAID's money. Therefore, without USAID — and given that Elon Musk has called it a "criminal organization responsible for deaths" — this funding for subversive activities will cease. This, in turn, is a blow to the entire global liberal environment. Essentially, it is a missile strike on the headquarters of globalism. And Trump and Musk made it happen.

The consequences, in my view, will be profoundly felt in all countries. We will suddenly realize that this oppressive pressure on our Russian society is coming to an end. It is no secret that USAID helped draft Yeltsin's Constitution in 1993, through which it controlled Russia.

Before that, it played a role in the collapse of the Soviet Union, laying the foundation for the creation of the Russian Federation, which was initially intended to be part of the global world under the direct control of USAID and the globalist elites.

Vladimir Putin began resisting this external control as soon as he came to power in 2000, focusing on strengthening sovereignty. However, USAID operated in Russia until 2012. It was only when Putin assumed his third presidential term that USAID was officially banned from Russia. Indirectly, of course, it continued to exert influence, as much of the political opposition and many representatives of the so-called "sixth column" remained closely tied to it. Only now is this coming to an end.

I must admit, this news is so significant that it is hard to comprehend. Until recently, we believed that globalists were a permanent fixture, that USAID was an almost eternal structure, and that the U.S. would always be the vanguard of globalization. We thought nothing could be done, and no one could change this. But it turns out that it can be changed — and it already has been.

TRUMP'S VISION: THE ORDER OF GREAT POWERS

WHAT TRUMP IS DOING upon returning to power in the U.S. is nothing short of staggering. He is rapidly and irreversibly reshaping the entire global order. In his first presidential term, Trump merely hinted at necessary reforms, but after four years in office and another four years in radical opposition, he has become a firm adherent of a well-defined ideology. Now, as evident from his first two weeks back in the White House, he is determined to implement this ideology at all costs.

What Is This Ideology?

The defining and fundamental characteristic of Trump's ideology is his unwavering opposition to globalism and liberalism — on all levels, in all spheres, and in every sense.

Trump is an enemy of globalism because he rejects all supranational institutions — be it the UN, WHO, or the European Union. Like classical realists in international relations, he believes that the highest authority is the sovereign nation-state, beyond which there is nothing and no one. This is the essence of his slogan "Make America Great Again." According to this worldview, the U.S. is, first and foremost, a Great Power that must act as a full-fledged political actor concerned solely with pursuing its own national interests, protecting its values, and ensuring its prosperity.

Trump and his ideology categorically reject any notion of internationalism, any rhetoric about so-called "universal human values," "world democracy," or "human rights." The sole absolute imperative is America and its well-being. Those who align with this vision are friends or allies; those who oppose it are enemies. The U.S. has no other mission beyond its own prosperity, and no external authority has the right to dictate to Americans what to do, how to behave, what to believe in, or whom to worship.

Globalism, in contrast, operates on the exact opposite logic. According to its tenets, the U.S. is meant to be the outpost, protector, and financier of liberal democracy, serving supranational interests and advancing ultra-liberal ideology — even at the expense of its own interests, and even engaging in self-reproach for having such interests at all. Globalists think in terms of humanity as a whole. Trump, however, thinks in terms of America. This reflects a fundamental divide in international relations theory — between realists (Trump) and liberals (Biden, as well as Obama, Clinton, and even Republican George W. Bush).

Furthermore, Trump radically rejects liberalism as an ideology of gender fluidity, progressivism, hyper-individualism, and postmodernism. On this level, he positions himself as a classical conservative, firmly defending traditional values — two divinely ordained and natural genders (male and female), the family as a cornerstone of society, religion, discipline, self-reliance, optimism, and a rejection of moral relativism, legalized perversions, and the forced imposition of collective guilt. He opposes the culture of cancellation, liberal censorship, and the dismantling of all forms of collective identity.

Liberalism, on the other hand, has transformed these issues into a quasi-religious cult, a sectarian dogma in which even the slightest criticism of LGBT or transgender ideology is immediately branded as "fascism," leading to punitive measures by the liberal establishment.

Thus, Trump's ideology is in complete and fundamental opposition to the geopolitical and ideological trajectory that has dominated the U.S. since the 1980s. This trajectory has been based on liberal progressivism, which insists that the individual must be increasingly freed from all social ties and obligations — including not just gender distinctions but even human nature itself (hence the rise of cyborg discourse and post-humanism). In global politics, this meant a gradual transition from nation-states toward a One World system under a global government, with the parallel abolition of national sovereignty — akin to the modern European Union model.

Trump has decisively rejected both liberal ideology and the geopolitics of globalism. Not only has he rejected them, but he has set out to reshape world reality with relentless energy, dramatically altering nearly everything within just two weeks of returning to the White House.

A World Rejected and a World Rebuilt

The world that Trump is dismantling is well understood — it is the world envisioned and built by globalists. Its parameters are clear, its methods known, and its logical trajectory foreseeable. But Trump has severed this trajectory, and his actions now appear irreversible.

The question now is: what kind of world is Trump constructing in its place?

It would be tempting to describe his vision as multipolar — a world composed of civilizations, free from a single dominant ideology or geopolitical force, where nations and cultures, having cast off the yoke of globalism, can finally breathe and embark on sovereign civilizational development. This is the world order sought by Russia, China, India, the Islamic world, Africa, and Latin America, which is precisely why they have united under the BRICS framework.

Perhaps, in practice, Trump's reforms will lead to this outcome. However, he does not appear to frame it in these terms. Trump is unlikely to consciously embrace multipolarity, even though some of his allies, such as Marco Rubio, have already acknowledged multipolarity as an objective reality. While this would satisfy many nations, Trump himself does not seem ready to accept it.

Instead, Trump appears to envision a *final rupture with both the Yalta system and the unipolar globalist moment.* He has therefore set out to dismantle all international institutions that symbolize the past eighty years — the UN, globalist structures like the WHO and USAID, and even NATO.

Trump sees *the United States as a new empire,* and himself as a modern Augustus, who formally ended the decaying Republic. His ambitions extend beyond America itself — hence his interest in acquiring Greenland, Canada, the Panama Canal, and even Mexico.

In Trump's eyes, the U.S. is the ultimate Great Power, the embodiment of humanity's highest aspirations — but a self-contained one, a shining ideal on a hill, admired and feared by all, accountable to no one. America owes nothing to anyone; it is not a universal donor but a global actor in its own right. It does not replace humanity but represents its most exceptional part — the most efficient, successful, wealthy, free, and prosperous society on Earth.

To join this elite world, one must make an effort. This explains Trump's hostility towards illegal immigration. The U.S. is not an open gateway for the lazy and unskilled to leech off welfare while scorning traditional values. Being American is a privilege and a mark of distinction. Others may admire or resent the U.S. from afar — it is irrelevant. But should anyone challenge this colossus, the full force of the American military machine will crush them.

For Trump, the goal is not Western hegemony but *exclusive American hegemony.* This is not an acceptance of multipolarity but a reimagined unipolarity, built on radically different principles than those of liberals and globalists.

Trump's America and the Fate of Europe

Trump's vision translates domestically into the *dismantling of the globalist liberal elite,* likely through a forceful purge. He himself has faced persecution, political harassment, and even assassination attempts. He knows that the scale of his reforms leaves him no room for hesitation — any misstep could allow his enemies to reclaim control. That is why he strikes first, systematically eliminating his opponents within the U.S. He has already begun this process — and he will not stop.

Regarding Europe, Trump likely holds overwhelmingly negative views. His closest ally, Elon Musk, recently declared "Make Europe Great Again" (MEGA) — a call for the overthrow of Euro-globalist elites and the rise of right-wing populists, the *Euro-Trumpists.*

But Trump himself does not seem to believe in a "great Europe." A strong Europe would compete with the U.S., and, more importantly, the EU remains dominated by the very globalist elites that Trump is uprooting at home. The European Union is both an ideological adversary and a geopolitical competitor. If Europe aspires to become a Great Power, that is its own affair. Trump's priority is America, not strengthening its rivals.

Thus, he would rather dismantle Europe, reverting it to a system of sovereign nation-states rather than consolidating its unity. This presents a dilemma for Euro-Trumpists — they oppose the Euro-globalist elite but are also European patriots who want to see a strong, sovereign, and independent Europe. To be like Trump's America does not mean being a mere tool of Trump's America.

The lesson is clear: liberal-globalist elites must be overthrown to achieve full ideological and geopolitical European sovereignty. But for Europe to be truly sovereign, it must counterbalance the new American hegemony.

This is Trump's ultimate message: *be sovereign!* That is America's law, and for it to become Europe's law, Europeans must rely on their own strength — not blindly follow the U.S. but build their own independent alliances and coalitions. Thus, Euro-Trumpism will inevitably discover multipolarity. In this world, America is a hegemon, but there is also room for other sovereign actors.

Trump desires sovereignty for America — but by example, he invites others to reject globalist liberalism and claim sovereignty for themselves. Hence, the transition from MAGA to MEGA.

Trump and Putin's Russia

How will Putin's Russia react to Trump?

While Russia recognizes the validity of Trump's opposition to globalism, there will be no concessions on sovereignty. Russia has already defended its sovereignty against the *entire collective West* when it was fully controlled by globalists. With the West now divided, Moscow will cling to sovereignty even more firmly. But so will Trump. He has his empire; Russia has its own.

They may clash, but in an entirely new context — *a world of Great Powers beyond globalism.*

The Biggest Loser: China

Under Trump, China will suffer the most. Until now, Beijing has skillfully balanced globalism and sovereignty, leveraging both to maximize economic gains while strengthening its independence as a Great Power. The extent to which China's rise depended on globalization remains uncertain, but that will soon become clear — because Trump intends to *sever all avenues for China to continue its previous course.*

Trump sees China as the main competitor to American hegemony and has already launched a new phase of economic and trade warfare against it — far more aggressively than even the Biden administration. Trump will attempt to eradicate the profits China has drawn from the U.S. and its global influence.

China will undoubtedly remain sovereign and, therefore, a Great Power. But it will now face much harsher conditions, in direct opposition to the United States.

For Trump, Russia is not a primary threat — but China is. As a result, the center of gravity in U.S. foreign policy will shift away from Russia and toward China.

After China, the most problematic region for Trump will be the Middle East. Unlike many American realists (such as John Mearsheimer and Jeffrey Sachs), he maintains a strictly pro-Israel orientation. To Trump, Israel is a miniature version of the United States, and the hardline right-wing politician Netanyahu is his alter ego, a reflection of Emperor Trump himself.

This makes Iran, the Shiite world, and the Axis of Resistance — the anti-Israel coalition of Islamic nations and the Palestinians — his natural enemies. How far Trump will go in his Middle Eastern policy remains uncertain, but as a modern Augustus, he views Israel as a *sacred and chosen colony*. Its enemies are his enemies.

Thus, the idea of Iran becoming a Great Power or the Islamic Ummah uniting into a singular political-religious entity is unlikely to appeal to Trump. During his first term, he expressed strong anti-Islamic sentiments, although he later softened his rhetoric. However, the very notion of an Islamic power center and an Islamic revival is something he fundamentally opposes.

One thing is certain: "Make Islam Great Again" is not part of Trump's plans. But it very well could be part of the plans of the Islamic world itself. If everyone around them is striving for greatness, why should not Muslims pursue the same path?

Trump and the Rising Great Powers: India, Latin America, and Africa

If Russia is a secondary issue for Trump and China is his greatest rival, then India, which is now clearly on its own path to becoming a Great Power, appears to Trump as a natural ally and friend.

Here, two factors play a role:

1) Regional competition with China

2) Tensions with the Islamic world.

In Modi, Trump sees a kindred spirit — a right-wing leader committed to sovereignty and traditional values. Thus, "Make India Great Again" (MIGA) seems entirely acceptable to Trump.

Meanwhile, Latin America is a source of irritation for Trump simply by its existence. It is the origin of waves of illegal migrants, drug cartels, and criminal gangs. The growing Latino population threatens to erode WASP (White Anglo-Saxon Protestant) identity in the U.S. This is why Trump is determined to build his Wall — beyond it lies a territory of chaos, crime, decadence, and backwardness. He does not see Latin America in terms of "greatness."

However, Latin America itself may think differently. The collapse of globalism in the U.S. creates new opportunities for Latin America. If the world is moving toward greatness, why should Latin American nations not follow this path? Trump may oppose it, but this is a matter of principle. Sooner or later, movements will emerge proclaiming: "Let's Make Latin America Great Again!"

Finally, there is Africa — a region with weaker international integration. However, Trump has already made his position clear. He has strongly condemned the expropriation of White-owned farmland by indigenous African populations in South Africa, even threatening harsh retaliatory measures.

Clearly, the Pan-African idea of "Making Africa Great Again" and permanently breaking with its colonial past will not find support from Trump. However, that does not mean it will be stopped.

Trump's Unintended Contribution to Multipolarity

Paradoxically, the new post-liberal world order that Trump is building is leading — objectively — to multipolarity.**

By declaring his ambition to make America a great wower, Trump has inadvertently opened the door for others to do the same — both established Great Powers (Russia, China, India) and aspiring ones. Europe may seek to reclaim its place as a Great Power. The Islamic world, Latin America, and even Africa may also set their sights on sovereignty and geopolitical prominence.

Though this goal may still be distant, the conditions of post-global geopolitics are pushing all other regions in this direction.

Whether Trump *wants it or not*, he is ushering in an era of Great Powers.

And in doing so, he is accelerating the rise of a multipolar world — even if he himself sees no further than a new form of American hegemony, a purified and explicitly imperial version of unipolarity.

Yes, BRICS irritates him, and he has even threatened to impose tariffs as a response to any attempt to introduce a new global reserve currency, warning of consequences for challenging the dominance of the dollar in world trade. However, at the same time, he is actively promoting the token economy, Bitcoin, and even meme coins, which in essence represent a break from the monopoly on financial issuance.

That is why we should not focus solely on individual statements, gestures, or even specific political steps taken by Trump, but rather on the *ideological and geopolitical model* he follows. And above all, we must take into account its antagonism and fundamental opposition to the liberal globalism that has dominated both the U.S. and the world until very recently.

Trump symbolically *opens the era of Great Powers*. With the fall of the globalists and the end of their absolute rule over world politics, *entirely new horizons* are emerging.

The Black Book of Liberalism

With Trump's rapid reforms — declaring that only two sexes exist, male and female — a *terrifying picture* has suddenly emerged before the eyes of Americans and the entire world. Millions of people who had been deceived by the liberal elites that previously ruled, who changed their sex or identified with non-existent genders, have now gone from being the so-called "progressive vanguard of society" to *cripples and invalids*.

Until just recently, they were indoctrinated to believe that diversity and gender transition, including castration, mutilation, and the psychological destruction of young children, were signs of the most rational and socially acceptable behavior. But now it has suddenly been revealed that those who promoted this ideology were nothing but maniacs and criminals, and those who followed it were victims, who *voluntarily turned themselves into monstrosities.*

Liberals almost drove their societies into the abyss, all while telling them lullaby-like lies to keep them complacent. But Trump instantly exposed the truth — the abyss was real, and many had already fallen into it.

Many parents have already physically, psychologically, and socially destroyed their children, losing them forever. Even Elon Musk himself suffered from this, as his child was turned into an imbecile. They will never recover from this.

What the liberals have done is nothing short of a massive social experiment — one even more horrifying than Nazism and Communism.

And this is not just a gang of maniacs, perverts, pedophiles, and schizophrenics — it is an entire *ideology* that has taken its core principle to the extreme: *the absolute negation of all forms of collective identity in favor of radical individualism.*

I discussed this with Tucker Carlson. He was horrified by what was happening in the West. And now, Tucker Carlson is in the White House. Trump has sharply halted the psycho-physical genocide of the American people.

How do transgender people, drag queens, "body positivity" activists, the mutilated, the castrated, the quadrubears feel now?

Especially the trans-children, who have suddenly gone from being the celebrated heroes of woke culture to outcasts and victims of inhuman perversion...

How are they supposed to study, live, build families, when the new, healthy generation of the Trump era — where there are only two sexes — will see them as biological waste, as mental and physical degenerates?

It is time to compile the "Black Book of Liberalism." Because this is about ideology. Liberalism must be recognized as a criminal and extremist ideology.

It is responsible for terrorism, wars, coups, genocide, orchestrated deception by international media, color revolutions, assassinations, and, most horrifyingly, the mass violence and psychological trauma inflicted upon hundreds of thousands — perhaps millions — of children who have suffered irreparable harm to their bodies and minds.

Liberals have mangled the souls and bodies of countless numbers of their own citizens.

And as for what the *elites* have done to defenseless migrant children, it is beyond imagination.

Now, the truth about the pedophile orgies of the U.S. Democratic Party elite is beginning to surface — the Satanic rituals held on Epstein's island, the P. Diddy parties in which many of them participated. Soon, all the details will be revealed.

And America will shudder — as will all of humanity.

Three Criminal Ideologies

All three Western political ideologies of the Modern Age have proven to be criminal, ultimately leading to bloody nightmares:

Communists destroyed entire social classes — the aristocracy, the peasantry — and slaughtered believers, cursing national identity and ancient traditions, all in the name of progress. In the end, it all collapsed into decay and ruin. And yet, this was a Western ideology, one that naive Russians fell for. *The Black Book of Communism* already exists.**

The horrors committed by the Nazis are widely known. Their memory has not faded, nor will it. And their ideological successors still exist today — the atrocities committed by Ukrainian Nazis against civilians are, unfortunately, yet another chapter in the "Black Book of Nazism."

Now, on a planetary scale, it is time to condemn liberalism as well — and *sentence it to death.*

Those who orchestrated all of this must face justice.

A Tribunal Is Coming

Stopping Western globalism and defeating this anti-human ideology, system, and political order should have been the duty of all humanity.

But instead, the system was overthrown from within.

The Americans themselves have toppled the deranged liberal elite and delivered their verdict.

A tribunal is coming. It is *inevitable.*

The Trumpists have dealt a crushing blow to the heart of the liberal octopus — USAID, the very system that financed global liberalism in all its forms: terrorism, extremism, corporate media, espionage, coups, assassinations, data falsification, persecution of dissidents.

In fact, USAID has been directly responsible for forming, financing, and politically supporting Ukrainian Nazism. But this is only the tip of the iceberg.

And now, a crucial realization:

All three Western ideologies of the Modern Age must be recognized as criminal.

Otherwise, we will wander aimlessly in a vicious cycle, moving from one criminal system to another.

Even now, there is no guarantee that the West, having rejected liberalism and despising communism, will not fall for nationalism again — and in its ugliest forms.

If that happens, the cycle will repeat itself once more.

We must break this cycle and move beyond it.

The Western Modern Age is not the only realm of political ideas and theories. There are many alternatives, including those that are neither Western nor Modern. All of this forms the ideological lexicon of the Fourth Political Theory.

Thus, the tribunal against liberalism and liberals must not push us back into fascism or communism. All three ideologies are criminal, failed, and inhuman. For none of them contain God, Christ, love, the soul, or the people as a historical subject. None of them offer the deep, authentic experience of Being. None of them recognize *Dasein*. They are all atheistic, materialistic, and alienating. They were designed to replace religion itself. But such an idea is already perverse, criminal, and a prelude to catastrophe. That is why Trump places such emphasis on religion. Let him have his faith — that is America's business.

As for us, we have our own faith. But beyond the Western Modern Age, we must all move *together*. We began the war against liberalism — both within our own country and in Ukraine. But the decisive blow was delivered by the Americans themselves.

TRUMP WALKS ACROSS
THE PLANET

This interview was originally published on 12 February 2025.

A Conversation That Never Happened

Tatiana Ladyaeva (Sputnik): The agenda is packed: according to American leader Donald Trump, a conversation took place between him and Vladimir Putin. Trump claims that the discussion was productive, yet the Kremlin neither confirmed nor denied this information.

Let us discuss whether we should know if this conversation actually took place — and why.

Alexander Dugin: There are solid reasons for the ambiguity surrounding the conversation between Putin and Trump.

First, Kremlin spokesman Dmitry Peskov denied the very fact of these negotiations, while Trump mentioned them reluctantly and only in passing. It is evident that such conversations did indeed occur, but perhaps they should be considered preliminary rather than full-fledged, as both we and the Americans — as well as the global community at large — are expecting the beginning of a strategic dialogue between these two leaders, representatives of the two key poles of the emerging multipolar system. This dialogue should address not only the situation in Ukraine but also the future of the global order.

This is a truly crucial issue, comparable to Yalta, where the fate of the world was decided. Expectations for this conversation are extremely high, and the outcome of these negotiations determines, if not everything, then almost everything. However, in the midst of these justified expectations, we hear reports that, in essence, the negotiations did not happen. Why is this? Despite the fact that discussions did take place, they have not yet fully begun in the true sense of the word. This was clearly something preliminary, related to an initial approach to the subject. It is premature to say that the conversation truly took place and that both sides understood each other.

The situation surrounding the Ukrainian conflict and our war against the collective West is so distorted in the media and in the reports of political analysts and experts in America that Trump has formed a completely false perception of what is happening in Ukraine and the causes of this conflict. He is, in fact, poorly informed about the situation. Nevertheless, he wants to resolve this issue quickly and move on, so he can focus on more pressing problems for himself: purging the Democratic Party and finalizing the shift in the balance of power within the U.S. He has global geopolitical plans concerning other regions — such as the Panama Canal, Greenland, Gaza, and others. But Ukraine concerns him the least; he would prefer for this problem to disappear. It is likely that he proposed some sort of solution to Vladimir Putin that seemed acceptable to him.

However, without delving into the details and without understanding history, geopolitics, ethnology, religious issues, or the vast array of lies imposed on the Ukrainian issue by the collective West, it is impossible to solve all these problems with a single stroke. Moreover, Trump chose an entirely unsuitable figure to conduct these negotiations — Kellogg. He is an old-school figure with a primitive view of how negotiations should proceed: "I say — you do. We command — you obey."

Tatiana Ladyaeva (Sputnik): So, he is not going to consider any deeper issues or take them into account?

Alexander Dugin: Just look at Kellogg's face, and you will understand that people with such external features and facial expressions usually do not delve into details. They act straightforwardly, like an outdated tank that is incapable of maneuvering and simply moves along a predetermined trajectory. This creates serious problems, as in other matters Trump relies on new, flexible people who have a deep understanding of ongoing processes.

I would recommend, for example, Steve Bannon to handle this issue. He is an intellectual and ideologue close to Trump, who held the position of National Security Advisor in the first administration. Bannon did a lot to help Trump get re-elected for a second term — effectively a third term, since it is now becoming evident that the previous election was simply stolen by the Democrats. There are also other figures who could deal with Russia-related issues.

Kellogg is a very unfortunate choice. Apparently, due to this, as well as Trump's lack of a clear understanding of the essence of the conflict, a misunderstanding occurred. What our president said or hinted at regarding how we envision victory and the conditions for negotiations or a ceasefire is so clear that even if Putin merely hinted at the minimal conditions for beginning a dialogue with America on Ukraine — because Ukraine itself is not a subject — this could have shocked Trump. He may have proposed something that seemed very good and acceptable to him but turned out to be completely unacceptable to us.

Because of this, it is difficult for us to assess the very fact of these negotiations. It seems like they took place, but in essence, they did not. It is both true and not true. This is a very delicate moment. Perhaps that is why we do not want to draw much attention to covering this half-accomplished fact in our society — because nothing is ready yet. Expectations are enormous. We could ruin everything with one wrong word or an incautious metaphor from some short-sighted analyst. Therefore, in my opinion, it is better not to know for now.

To answer your question: there are times when, given the immense public scrutiny on delicate and fragile negotiations between two world leaders — on whose conversation the fate of humanity and the entire architecture of the still-developing multipolarity depends — it is wiser to step aside for a bit and focus on something else.

Zelensky Is a Nobody

Tatiana Ladyaeva (Sputnik): Over the past two to three years, we have perhaps become accustomed to baseless statements by politicians and leaders, which are not followed by real actions — and sometimes even by completely opposite steps. Often, we continue living as if nothing happened. However, returning to the current situation: Zelensky, likely against the backdrop of potential negotiations between Putin and Trump, declares his readiness for any format of dialogue. The key point for him remains security guarantees from Washington. What exactly these guarantees entail — NATO membership, military bases, financial aid — is still unclear. How can such statements be interpreted?

Alexander Dugin: Zelensky undoubtedly realizes that his time is running out, and with it, the history of Ukraine comes to an end. The war that broke out, along with all the provocations and acts of terror, was initiated by the previous administration. The current U.S. leadership does not intend to continue this policy of support, and therefore, Zelensky finds himself in a dead-end situation. His desperate attempts to intervene in the situation resemble a frog trying to climb out of a bucket of milk. He seeks to draw attention to himself despite the fact that no one is asking him and no negotiations are being conducted with him. The main discussions will be centered on the strategic dialogue between Putin and Trump, concerning not only Ukraine but also the global order.

Zelensky is trying to assert his presence, emphasizing his role as a leader with terrorist structures under his control. However, this appears to be nothing more than a desperate attempt to attract attention. He is ready to return to his roots in Kvartal 95,[1] doing everything pos-

---

1   Ed. note: Kvartal 95 is a Ukrainian entertainment and production company founded by Volodymyr Zelenskyy, originally as a comedy troupe in the early 2000s. It became famous for political satire and produced the hit TV series *Servant of the People*, in which Zelenskyy played a teacher who becomes president — a role that foreshadowed his real-life election in 2019. Though he

sible to stay relevant. But interest in him will wane with each passing day — both from Washington and other participants in the conflict.

At this moment, Washington views Zelensky as a burden. His role in the context of U.S.-Russia negotiations needs to be determined, but so far, he has no significant influence. It is quite possible that Washington will decide it does not need this figure in its plans. In response, Zelensky is demonstrating his willingness to make any concessions. Previously, he refused negotiations, but now he is ready to discuss any options. If he were offered to come to Moscow and meet with Putin, he would agree, though his speech might be incomprehensible to most.

We are now witnessing a different version of Zelensky — a more compliant one, ready for compromises. However, he will continue to speak in his own language for his supporters, which may not be understood by a wider audience. This is irrelevant to us; what matters is completing the special military operation, liberating Novorossiya and Kiev, and ideologically cleansing Ukraine from the Nazi regime. After that, we must begin building a new multipolar world in dialogue with all major players on the international stage.

Our goal is to engage not only with the West and Trump but also with Europe, which is now clearly deviating from its previous course. This could become a serious challenge. At the same time, we continue our cooperation with China, India, the Islamic world, Africa, and Latin America. This is the *essence of building a multipolar world*, in which Ukraine has no place.

The role of this aggressive Anti-Russia, artificially created on our borders and within our united Russian world, was intended to prevent the formation of a multipolar world. However, this process has already begun, and we are actively participating in it. Thus, Zelensky has no prospects. He may be replaced or used for certain tactical moves, but the illusion that Kiev has independent agency has already vanished, and all sides are now fully aware of this.

---

stepped away from the company after taking office, Kvartal 95 remains a major media force in Ukraine.

USAID, the Russian Constitution, and the Sixth Column

Tatiana Ladyaeva (Sputnik): Before moving on to the next topic, let's briefly address some listener questions. Mikhail, from the Radio Sputnik group on VKontakte, asks: "Given the official confirmation of USAID's involvement in the collapse of the Soviet Union, shouldn't we reconsider the [Russian] Constitution, which was drafted with their participation, and instead take as a model the market-socialist system of China, based on traditional principles?" I should note that the current Constitution has already undergone several amendments, adapting to modern realities. But what other aspects should we consider?

Alexander Dugin: In fact, this is an entirely logical question. Today, after Trump's Conservative Revolution, we are beginning to *fully grasp* the events that have unfolded over the past 35 years, especially since the 1990s. The scale of the catastrophe and the betrayal by the previous elites is now undeniable. It is therefore essential to identify those individuals who collaborated with the intelligence services of a hostile state and facilitated the establishment of external control over Russia in the 1990s. This concerns not only ideology, education, and law but also the Constitution itself. These individuals must be named and brought into the public eye. We must put an end to this history of external governance by a hostile civilization. Even if Trump strengthens his position (which is quite likely), this does not mean that we should follow America — neither liberal nor conservative America. We have our own destiny.

For 25 years, Vladimir Putin has worked to correct the terrible mistakes and consequences that led to the collapse of the Soviet Union and the destruction of our ideology, system, and industry in the 1990s. The 2000s were spent under the slogan: "We are moving away from the '90s, away from the '90s." We overcame those difficulties, removed their influence, and changed the elites. We gradually eliminated those who fled abroad and became open enemies of the state. This was a long and difficult process. However, it has now become clear that the Russian Federation's system of the 1990s was built with the direct involvement of USAID. It was a spy construct, designed for colonization and external control over our country.

We continue to dismantle this legacy. Now, with all the facts exposed, it is evident what Putin has been doing for the past 25 years. Many failed to notice how carefully the reforms were carried out to restore Russia's sovereignty. But now everything is becoming clear — and at the same time, we see how much remains to be done and how incomplete this process still is. We have eliminated the Fifth Column, but the Sixth Column remains. These are the same people who worked for USAID until 2012, when the organization was officially banned.

Beyond USAID, there were many other foundations and affiliates that penetrated our institutions, clubs, and international organizations with the goal of exerting control over us. Now, this picture is becoming undeniably clear, and the deeply embedded Sixth Column is finally coming under scrutiny. Their actions can no longer be justified as naive goodwill towards the Western world, because that very world is now waging a brutal war against us, splitting our Russian world in two. They have become accomplices in a crime. The Sixth Column is not just misguided liberals from the 1990s and 2000s — they are, in essence, *state criminals.*

Trump is identifying his own state criminals in the West, and we must take action on our own side, because there is *no longer any justification for maintaining this status quo.*

The Second Term Is Not the First

Tatiana Ladyaeva (Sputnik): Now, let's continue addressing listener questions submitted via the Radio Sputnik mobile app. Dmitry rightly points out the need to liberate Kursk Oblast, while Andrey suggests that Zelensky may face "absolute silence" in Moscow — although, of course, this remains speculation. Another listener asks about Trump's position on USAID: "If Trump knew about USAID's activities during his first term, why is the investigation only starting now?" May I offer my opinion? Perhaps Trump's second presidential term is fundamentally different from the first for several reasons.

Alexander Dugin: That's absolutely correct. Trump's first term can be seen as a preliminary stage, a trial run. It was a *technical failure* in the functioning of liberal globalism. Nevertheless, Trump demonstrated that an opponent of liberal globalism could actually win — even in the United States. This was a *genuine shock.*

He entered office alone, confronting a system that was fundamentally opposed to him. Trump aimed to "drain the swamp" and change the dominant ideology in the United States — though he wasn't able to fully achieve this in his first term. However, he laid the groundwork, assembled a team, and became a charismatic leader for the *majority of Americans.* He also initiated a crucial dialogue with high-tech elites — specifically conservative-oriented Silicon Valley oligarchs like Elon Musk and Peter Thiel. This new strategic shift allowed him to secure critical support by 2024, ultimately leading to his victory.

Now, he has brought these people into key positions within his new administration. He has begun a *true revolution.*

If he failed to "drain the swamp" the first time, now he has struck directly at the monstrous beast lurking at its center. In reality, this is no longer just a political battle — it is a war. A war against formidable opponents, and USAID is just the beginning. Next, Trump plans to audit the Pentagon and the CIA, effectively dismantle the Department of Education, and reform the Federal Reserve System. He has cut off one head of the Hydra, but many more remain, which must be dealt with by Elon Musk, DOGE, and Ron Paul.

This is a *monumental revolution* — perhaps even more significant than 1991, or even 1917 in our country. This is a complete paradigm shift. Minus turns into plus, black turns into white. Of course, some may believe that white is turning into black, but this is an unmistakable 180-degree turn. USAID was the first head of the Hydra to be severed — and as Elon Musk put it, "there is no restoring it." But now, all the remaining heads must be dealt with. The Democrats are panicking, screaming, and demanding a return to the past, even threatening civil war. Let's see how this unfolds.

MEGA — Loyal Metropolises

Tatiana Ladyaeva (Sputnik): Let's turn to major events in Europe. In Madrid, the third-largest summit of the European Parliament political group Patriots for Europe took place. The meeting was attended by right-wing leaders from EU countries, including Hungarian Prime Minister Viktor Orbán, French opposition leader Marine Le Pen, and others. The agreements reached deserve special attention: summit participants expressed their support for the policies of U.S. President Donald Trump, opposed further aid to Ukraine, and spoke out against radical Islam, illegal immigration, gender diversity, and the "green" agenda. Alexander Gelyevich [Dugin], how realistic are these plans?

Alexander Dugin: You undoubtedly understand that if the situation remains as it is and the status quo persists, conservative forces will remain merely a wishful-thinking faction of relatively minor influence in the broader European context. It is important to note that Trumpists, who share similar positions on key issues such as geopolitics, illegal immigration, the green agenda, and gender diversity, were initially perceived as marginal figures — outcasts, pariahs. Before Trump's victory and his inauguration, they were mocked and labeled as "extremists," "far-right," or even "fascists." However, in the end, a Conservative Revolution triumphed in America, and these so-called "marginals" became part of the ruling power.

Power has truly shifted.

Europe, long accustomed to being part of the Atlantic community, now finds itself in a state of confusion. On the one hand, the "provinces" are witnessing the rise of entirely different forces in the "metropolis." On the other hand, they are still not ready to fully acknowledge Trump's correctness. Nevertheless, an opposition is emerging, one ideologically aligned with Trump, preparing for a European Conservative Revolution.

At this moment, this opposition has significant backing from across the ocean. Elon Musk has announced the launch of the MEGA project — *Make Europe Great Again* — modeled after the MAGA movement, *Make America Great Again.* He has reconfigured influence networks previously controlled by globalists, such as those tied to Soros, redirecting them to support this revolution. This is reminiscent of the actions of the Bolsheviks, who seized control of the post office and telegraph, thus initiating their own communication networks among their supporters. A similar takeover is now occurring within key centers of power in America (and, by extension, throughout the Western world) by conservative investment groups aligned with Trumpists.

Thus, the seizure of key management centers in America by conservative investment groups loyal to Trumpists is underway. They have begun to support European right-wing parties such as Alternative for Germany (AfD) and leaders like Orbán and the Italian conservatives Salvini and Meloni. Marine Le Pen is also receiving backing from these new forces.

While the power dynamics in the "metropolis" have changed, the "provinces" remain bewildered. Many political forces that had been marginalized and repressed until recently are now beginning to gain popularity. Liberal fascism, in this context, has worked in reverse: those who accused their opponents of tyranny and racism turned out to be the true dictators and racists. Now, the MEGA movement is rising — an alternative Europe oriented towards traditional values and opposed to anti-traditional ideologies.

It can be argued that we are on the brink of a European Conservative Revolution. Its first representatives are becoming active and organizing. At present, they constitute the third-largest political group in the European Parliament. Although, apart from a few countries like Hungary, Slovakia, and Italy — with their leaders Viktor Orbán and Giorgia Meloni — they have not yet come to power, the presence of

Trumpists on the European political stage is a significant achievement, given that they have the backing of the United States under Trump's leadership.

On the other hand, in countries where they have not yet gained power — such as France, Germany, and Spain — conservatives still enjoy massive public support. However, the liberal elite maintains a stranglehold on political mechanisms, ensuring that this fact remains largely unspoken. Conservatives are subjected to what is known as "canceling" — they are essentially "canceled," yet they represent the majority. Therefore, only a slight push is needed for the European Union and its globalist elite to begin to crumble.

I believe that Macron and Scholz are candidates for removal. How this will happen — whether through political or democratic means — is no longer of paramount importance. When a revolutionary situation arises, it is resolved either peacefully or violently.

How events will unfold is still difficult for me to predict. This is, in a sense, the first attempt. Previously, they gathered as a club of the rejected — pariahs, *chandala*, who met in anticipation of the next wave of repression. But now, it is something different. Now, they are representatives of a new Trumpist conservative-revolutionary bloc with serious backing from across the ocean. This is the main force in the West, making the situation highly interesting.

It is important to note that these forces are strongly sympathetic to Russia. Among them are those who fully support us, those who waver, and even those who have betrayed us in the past — like Meloni in a different geopolitical situation. We will remember this: her actions were dishonorable and deceitful, as she effectively participated in a war against us. Nevertheless, considering the broader picture, European right-wing populists are friendly towards Trump and are also oriented toward Russia's traditional values.

This represents an intriguing phenomenon. We have never worked with these forces before. We are traditional internationalists and, by inertia, consider ourselves leftists, having engaged with leftist groups in the West or with those in power. But neither approach has yielded results. The left has practically degenerated: today, they are merely involved in pride parades and advocating migrants, while their leadership has become those with whom we now find ourselves in conflict.

If we speak of potential allies in Europe, the most suitable representatives for cooperation with us are the forces behind the *Make Europe Great Again* movement. These conservative groups fundamentally share our traditional values. They oppose the green agenda and abstract demands that undermine our national culture and economy. They oppose illegal immigration, support the traditional family structure, and reject gender ideology — positions that we also uphold.

It is difficult to find significant differences between us and these forces, apart from their Russophobia and active actions against us. This is undoubtedly a serious factor that we cannot ignore. However, if they begin to show sympathy towards Russia and adopt a friendly stance in this new stage of relations, the situation could change. For example, Viktor Orbán has already done much to shift Western perceptions of Russia. What has previously repelled us was their Russophobia and open hostility, which remains a significant factor that we will not forget. However, should they start displaying friendship and goodwill towards Russia in this new geopolitical context, it may alter our perspective — especially if they follow their new allies in Washington.

It is essential to understand that a truly sovereign Europe should not be merely a compliant instrument in American hands. We may soon witness the formation of two competing poles within the West, two sovereign entities capable of rivaling each other. However, for now, the liberal elite, comprised of radical Russophobes and racists waging war against us, continues to dominate Europe. Right-wing populists can be viewed as a potential fifth column in Europe. We previously paid them little attention, considering them marginal and extremist forces, but they represent the future — a future that will inevitably arrive in Europe.

With the loss of their main support in Washington, the left-liberal province of Europe may fracture, leading to processes akin to those occurring in America itself. A Conservative Revolution in Europe will gain momentum and consolidate. The only question is how long it will take and whether it will happen democratically or through violent upheavals — coup d'état, bloodshed, or civil war. In any case, we are prepared to accept any outcome, whether peaceful or radical.

A Toxic "Gift"

Tatiana Ladyaeva (Sputnik): I remind listeners that during Hungary's presidency of the European Parliament, Viktor Orbán made significant efforts, including personal meetings and repeated negotiations with Vladimir Putin. Furthermore, in two weeks, on February 23, Germany will hold parliamentary elections, which may lead to Olaf Scholz's resignation. Who will replace him remains an open question. Returning to the topic of *Make Europe Great Again*, let's consider a comment from Galina in our VKontakte group: "Donald Trump is trying to shift the responsibility for Ukraine's security onto Europe. Can Europe achieve greatness while bearing such obligations?" Can Europe truly become great under such burdens?

Alexander Dugin: Handing over a half-decayed, toxic corpse, exuding radiation and stench, is hardly a worthy gift for one's allies and friends. In this context, Ukraine appears to be just such a toxic waste. Trump is seemingly eager to rid himself of this burden. If Europe is left to face Russia alone, the collapse of the globalist liberal elite will accelerate. Thus, the *Trojan gift* — the assignment of responsibility to Europe for waging war against Russia in Ukraine — is presumably Trump's strategy to quickly weaken, and possibly even dismantle, his trade competitors while undermining his ideological opponents in Europe. The European elite openly opposes Trumpism.

For example, when Trump suggested the annexation of Greenland, Denmark responded by declaring its willingness to fight. Simply astonishing! Add to this Ukraine, with its decaying society and a frenzied population driven to a state of subhuman aggression — filled with rage towards everyone, clamoring for money and weapons — this terrorist entity reveals the clear reality that the responsibility for this conflict will fall squarely on the shoulders of the European Union.

If the EU assumes responsibility for Ukraine, it will become the most effective way for Trump to rid himself of a toxic asset that shackles him and places him at a disadvantage in the ongoing redrawing of the geopolitical map. While this will not lead to Europe's greatness, it will instead hasten its disintegration. Trump is likely counting on precisely this, believing that the current Europe will be unable to maintain its integrity and sovereignty in the face of new challenges. In place of old Europe, something new may emerge — something more sovereign and, possibly, stronger.

The Middle East and Trump's Plans: Alarming

Tatiana Ladyaeva (Sputnik): In our remaining time, let's discuss the Middle East situation. Trump has suggested that the U.S. could purchase the Gaza Strip, establishing control and overseeing reconstruction with the participation of Arab nations. He has also warned that he may lose patience with the Israel-Hamas agreement, as Hamas threatens to abandon the ceasefire. What do these statements mean, and how could the situation develop?

Alexander Dugin: Trump unequivocally takes a staunchly pro-Israel stance, supporting Netanyahu. Unlike in other regions, where our positions do not directly clash with Trump's, the Middle East is an area where Russia's stance sharply diverges from his. Trump believes that Palestinians should be expelled from their historical lands, such as Gaza, and resettled in Egypt or Jordan. This proposal horrifies the leadership of these countries and suggests severe measures for cleansing the West Bank.

In this scenario, Trump effectively greenlights Netanyahu's far-right government, which is ready to act without regard for Palestinian interests. For Trump, Hamas is an extremist organization, and therefore, he does not recognize Palestinians as legitimate subjects of international relations.

These plans amount to a catastrophe for Palestinians and are entirely unacceptable to the broader Islamic world. In this regard, I believe Trump is making his first major geopolitical miscalculation in shaping a new world order in the Middle East. He is alienating the Islamic world — a powerful force that he fails to recognize as an independent geopolitical pole. This is especially true regarding his antagonism towards Iran and the Shiite factions that maintain staunchly anti-Zionist and anti-Israeli positions.

Trump has firmly chosen Israel's side and is likely to pursue this course aggressively. At this moment, he is riding a wave of success, having already shattered many seemingly insurmountable barriers in American politics. This undoubtedly influences global affairs. He is emboldened and seemingly believes he can turn Gaza into a sort of Trump Tower.

Tatiana Ladyaeva (Sputnik): That's an interesting point, Alexander Gelyevich [Dugin]. Trump, as a businessman, approaches the situation in Gaza from a profit-oriented perspective. What makes this region so attractive for investment and business ventures?

Alexander Dugin: This area commands significant strategic importance due to its connection to trade routes linking the Indian Ocean and the Mediterranean. The key region is not Gaza itself but the surrounding territory, which plays a pivotal role in global trade and maritime routes. Trump believes that control over this region should belong to the United States. This explains his focus on the Panama Canal and similar strategic areas. It is a serious issue.

This involves global maritime communications. At the same time, it's crucial to note Trump's support for Netanyahu, whom he sees as a role model, similar to how he perceives Putin. Netanyahu, in Trump's eyes, is a strong, self-assured leader who achieves his goals by any means necessary. While such a comparison is unacceptable to us, Trump views Netanyahu as a charismatic figure leading the fight against radical Islam, towards which he has long harbored animosity. Trump appears willing to conduct bold experiments to construct *Greater Israel*.

However, he seems to underestimate the potential consequences of his actions, which could lead to an unprecedentedly bloody conflict in the Middle East. I hope that, despite his radical rhetoric and actions, once he fully assumes a role as a key global political architect, he will begin to take reality into account. Otherwise, he risks ending up like the liberals he ousted — those who ignored reality and sought to bend it to their will, only to see their globalist ideology collapse completely.

If Trump acts as paranoid as some of his predecessors, he could severely undermine his own position.

I've noticed an interesting shift: within Trump's support base, opinions on Israel are divided. It may seem that all Trumpists fully support Israel, but that is not the case. A significant portion of them back Israel, but this is only part of the movement — perhaps even less than half. Many conservative, right-wing defenders of traditional values within Trump's base do not unequivocally support the Israeli government. Notably, figures such as Tucker Carlson, Jeffrey Sachs, John Mearsheimer, and Candace Owens have openly criticized unconditional support for Netanyahu, condemning the mistreatment of Palestinians and denouncing the genocide.

Thus, the situation remains fluid and unstable. Our focus should be on Russia's interests — making Russia great, strengthening our sovereignty, and steadfastly adhering to the principles and ideals we hold true and just, without deviation under any circumstances.

OTHER BOOKS PUBLISHED BY ARKTOS

OTHER BOOKS PUBLISHED BY ARKTOS

	Pagan Imperialism
	Recognitions
	A Traditionalist Confronts Fascism
GUILLAUME FAYE	*Archeofuturism*
	Archeofuturism 2.0
	The Colonisation of Europe
	Convergence of Catastrophes
	Ethnic Apocalypse
	A Global Coup
	Prelude to War
	Sex and Deviance
	Understanding Islam
	Why We Fight
DANIEL S. FORREST	*Suprahumanism*
ANDREW FRASER	*Dissident Dispatches*
	Reinventing Aristocracy in the Age of Woke Capital
	The WASP Question
GÉNÉRATION IDENTITAIRE	*We are Generation Identity*
PETER GOODCHILD	*The Taxi Driver from Baghdad*
	The Western Path
PAUL GOTTFRIED	*War and Democracy*
PETR HAMPL	*Breached Enclosure*
PORUS HOMI HAVEWALA	*The Saga of the Aryan Race*
CONSTANTIN VON HOFFMEISTER	*Esoteric Trumpism*
	MULTIPOLARITY!
RICHARD HOUCK	*Liberalism Unmasked*
A. J. ILLINGWORTH	*Political Justice*
INSTITUT ILIADE	*For a European Awakening*
	Guardians of Heritage
ALEXANDER JACOB	*De Naturae Natura*
JASON REZA JORJANI	*Artemis Unveiled*
	Closer Encounters
	Erosophia
	Faustian Futurist
	Iranian Leviathan
	Lovers of Sophia
	Novel Folklore
	Philosophy of the Future
	Prometheism
	Promethean Pirate
	Prometheus and Atlas
	Psychotron
	Uber Man
	World State of Emergency
HENRIK JONASSON	*Sigmund*
EDGAR JULIUS JUNG	*The Significance of the German Revolution*
RUUBEN KAALEP & AUGUST MEISTER	*Rebirth of Europe*

OTHER BOOKS PUBLISHED BY ARKTOS

RODERICK KAINE	*Smart and SeXy*
JAMES KIRKPATRICK	*Conservatism Inc.*
LUDWIG KLAGES	*The Biocentric Worldview*
	Cosmogonic Reflections
	The Science of Character
ANDREW KORYBKO	*Hybrid Wars*
PIERRE KREBS	*Guillaume Faye: Truths & Tributes*
	Fighting for the Essence
JULIEN LANGELLA	*Catholic and Identitarian*
JOHN BRUCE LEONARD	*The New Prometheans*
DIANA PANCHENKO	*The Inevitable*
STEPHEN PAX LEONARD	*The Ideology of Failure*
	Travels in Cultural Nihilism
WILLIAM S. LIND	*Reforging Excalibur*
	Retroculture
PENTTI LINKOLA	*Can Life Prevail?*
GIORGIO LOCCHI	*Definitions*
H. P. LOVECRAFT	*The Conservative*
NORMAN LOWELL	*Imperium Europa*
RICHARD LYNN	*Sex Differences in Intelligence*
	A Tribute to Helmut Nyborg (ed.)
JOHN MACLUGASH	*The Return of the Solar King*
CHARLES MAURRAS	*The Future of the Intelligentsia &*
	For a French Awakening
JOHN HARMON MCELROY	*Agitprop in America*
MICHAEL O'MEARA	*Guillaume Faye and the Battle of Europe*
	New Culture, New Right
MICHAEL MILLERMAN	*Beginning with Heidegger*
DMITRY MOISEEV	*The Philosophy of Italian Fascism*
MAURICE MURET	*The Greatness of Elites*
BRIAN ANSE PATRICK	*The NRA and the Media*
	Rise of the Anti-Media
	The Ten Commandments of Propaganda
	Zombology
TITO PERDUE	*The Bent Pyramid*
	Journey to a Location
	Lee
	Morning Crafts
	Philip
	The Sweet-Scented Manuscript
	William's House (vol. 1–4)
JOHN K. PRESS	*The True West vs the Zombie Apocalypse*
RAIDO	*A Handbook of Traditional Living* (vol. 1–2)
P R REDDALL	*Towards Awakening*
CLAIRE RAE RANDALL	*The War on Gender*

OTHER BOOKS PUBLISHED BY ARKTOS

Steven J. Rosen	*The Agni and the Ecstasy*
	The Jedi in the Lotus
Nicholas Rooney	*Talking to the Wolf*
Richard Rudgley	*Barbarians*
	Essential Substances
	Wildest Dreams
Ernst von Salomon	*It Cannot Be Stormed*
	The Outlaws
Werner Sombart	*Traders and Heroes*
Piero San Giorgio	*Giuseppe*
	Survive the Economic Collapse
	Surviving the Next Catastrophe
Sri Sri Ravi Shankar	*Celebrating Silence*
	Know Your Child
	Management Mantras
	Patanjali Yoga Sutras
	Secrets of Relationships
George T. Shaw (ed.)	*A Fair Hearing*
Fenek Solère	*Kraal*
	Reconquista
Oswald Spengler	*The Decline of the West*
	Man and Technics
Richard Storey	*The Uniqueness of Western Law*
Tomislav Sunic	*Against Democracy and Equality*
	Homo Americanus
	Postmortem Report
	Titans are in Town
Askr Svarte	*Gods in the Abyss*
Hans-Jürgen Syberberg	*On the Fortunes and Misfortunes of Art in Post-War Germany*
Abir Taha	*Defining Terrorism*
	The Epic of Arya (2nd ed.)
	Nietzsche is Coming God, or the Redemption of the Divine
	Verses of Light
Jean Thiriart	*Europe: An Empire of 400 Million*
Bal Gangadhar Tilak	*The Arctic Home in the Vedas*
Dominique Venner	*Ernst Jünger: A Different European Destiny*
	For a Positive Critique
	The Shock of History
Hans Vogel	*How Europe Became American*
Markus Willinger	*A Europe of Nations*
	Generation Identity
Alexander Wolfheze	*Alba Rosa*
	Globus Horribilis
	Rupes Nigra

www.ingramcontent.com/pod-product-compliance
Lightning Source LLC
Chambersburg PA
CBHW021506090426
42739CB00007B/498